Tales of the Peanut Butter Kid, Again

Stories of a Colorado Farm Boy
Volume 2 of the Series
Adventures of the Peanut Butter Kid

Written and Illustrated
by Larry Wayne Miller

Tales of the Peanut Butter Kid, Again

First edition published in the United States of America in 2016.

Printed by Create Space, an Amazon.com Company.

eStore address   www.CreateSpace.com/6676084

Website: www.talesofthepeanutbutterkid.com
(Our website has a link to buy the book on Amazon)

Facebook: www.facebook.com/TalesofPeanutButterKid/

ISBN-10:   1539773000
ISBN-13:   978-1539773009

DEDICATION

Please enjoy the book!
Larry Wayne Miller

This book is dedicated to the hard-working Miller Family. The stories started here. In my early years, I sat at the feet of these people, listening and absorbing thousands of stories in the days before television and other new-fangled electronics.

--Larry Wayne Miller

Left to right:
Grandpa, Uncle Roy, Grandma, Aunt Mary,
Marion Miller (my dad), Aunt Coerene

TABLE OF CONTENTS

TALES OF THE PEANUT BUTTER KID, AGAIN

Go Kart   Page 4
Grandpa's New Tractor   Page 13
Flying!   Page 18
4/4 Time   Page 29
Humm Batta Batta   Page 41
Thanksgiving a la Peanut Butter   Page 51
Life in Black and White   Page 61
Fishin'   Page 75
Gleaning   Page 85
Sunset   Page 100
Three Men on a Slab   Page 109
Green Car Blue   Page 122
The Leroy Rule   Page 130
Plowing for Christmas   Page 139

GO KART

by Larry Wayne Miller

"Get outta my way!" Those were the last words I remember hearing on that fateful day in the summer of 1961. Oh, I did hear the scraping and the crunching. Oh, yes, and the crashing….I heard that, too, as I dove over the picket fence in front of our farm house, in Weldon Valley, Colorado.

It had all started a few weeks earlier with one tiny little innocent comment to my dad.

"Dad?" I said, sidling up to him while he worked at some bookkeeping on the kitchen table. He didn't answer, so I put my arm around him, patted his massive shoulder, and continued. "Dad, I've been thinking."

He didn't look at me, but he did turn to view my offending appendage resting on his arm. I quickly removed my hand and continued. "I've been thinking about cars."

Still no answer.

Undaunted, I tried one last tack. "I think it's time for me to get a sports car." *That* got his attention.

He carefully put down his pencil, looked straight ahead, and without making eye contact replied, "Son, you are only twelve years old."

"I know, Dad, but I'm mature for my age." That brought a snicker from my ten year old sister, Shirley. I ignored the irritating sibling and continued, "I've been driving a tractor since I was seven, and a truck since I was eight," I replied. "I think it's time to have my own wheels."

A vast vacuum seemed to suck the oxygen from the room. Mom discreetly left the premises, with the oxygen. Shirley left under protest.

"Here, Son, sit down," Dad said, motioning me to an empty chair.

I hated this part. It meant that he had already made up his mind, and I was about to be 'educated.' He leaned forward, and for the first time, looked me in the eye. He asked in a controlled tone, "You know that you can drive a tractor anytime you want, right?"

"I know, Dad, but I need something more

substantial," I said, feeling like I was being backed into a corner.

"I also let you drive the old blue truck on the back roads whenever you want," he said, obviously trying to understand.

"Yes, and I appreciate it," I said, trying to find the right words. "But, it's not a sports car."

He leaned back, with his arms still resting on the table, looking at me like I was an alien from outer space.

"Here, I'll show you," I said, reaching into my back pocket. I pulled out clippings from magazines, and drawings I had been making for the last month.

He slowly looked at all the evidence, pausing at my sketches. "You're pretty good with a pencil," he said, while looking at one of my drawings, in which I had combined all of the best elements of each sports car I'd seen.

"Thanks," I replied, feeling a little easing of the tension. After what seemed an eternity, he put all the papers down, and said, "What is this really about?"

"What do you mean?" I asked.

"What is it about a sports car that interests you the most?"

I thought for a few moments, and then replied, "Dad, trucks and tractors are *slow*, and I want to go *fast*." I had never consciously thought of it before, but that was the essence of it. Speed!

Dad's eyes lit up, and a knowing smile creased his face. "I know the feeling, Son," he said, gazing somewhere over my shoulder, lost in thought. "I felt the same way at your age." The smile turned into a grin as he continued. "Your Uncle Roy and I hopped up an old Model T truck once, and drove it all over the countryside, terrorizing our neighbors and the animals until your Grandpa found out." Dad's eyes danced with delight. "Oh, he was mad. I thought I would have to join the French Foreign Legion after that." He looked at me, and came back to the present. "So, you want speed, do you? We'll just have to see what we can do about that."

"Really?" I gushed.

He tipped his head and raised his eyebrows, "Within reason and prudence," he said. I understood one word but I never really got the hang of the other.

But, he understood! He really understood. Now we were in this together, and I knew that sometime soon I would go fast!

"Now let me finish this paperwork and we'll talk about this later," he said, shooing me out of the room.

I went outside and drove the Ford tractor as fast as it would go until dark. Fifteen miles an hour would have to do for now.

On Saturday, we finished evening chores early, and the whole family went to the fair at Fort Morgan. There was a Ferris Wheel and a Loop-the-Loop, and enough cotton candy to make all of us sick.

But what caught my eye was behind the Haunted House. There, running on a track laid out in used tires, were Go Karts! I had heard about them, but had never seen one in person. They were basically angle iron, tube steel, four rubber tires, with a four and a half horsepower engine. They weren't much to look at, but boy, could they go fast!

My heart started racing just watching them. Luckily, I hadn't spent any of my ride money, so I bought a ticket, got into a cart that looked fast, and listened to the driving instructions while Mom, Dad, and Shirley watched.

As soon as they let us start, I knew this would be FUN! It wasn't just that I was going fast, it was that I was a few inches above the ground and going fast.

After a few laps, I got the hang of it, and after a few more, the ride was over, and way too soon. What a waste of money! But I was hooked, and had just enough money for one more ride.

As I got in line, Shirley came and stood behind me. "What do you want?" I snarled.

"I'm going to ride, too," she beamed, as she held out her ticket to show me.

"Okay," I said, grudgingly. "But don't get in my way." She folded her arms and pouted, but her lips were turned up in a devilish grin.

I turned my attention to the Go Karts to see which one was fastest, while the line inched forward between rides. I determined that Number 33 was by far the fastest cart, so I arranged to get it, even letting a few people go ahead of me so I could be the first person in line when our turn came.

At last the gate opened, and I headed for my chosen Go Kart. There it was, Number 33! I got in, and impatiently waited for the instructions to end. Shirley got into some cart in the rear. That was fine. I didn't want to have to pass her, anyway.

Finally, we were off. But something very strange happened. People began passing me. I looked back at my number to check. It was Number 33....but it was *Green* Number 33! It was supposed to be *Blue* Number 33! Why would *anyone* have two Number 33's on the same race course?

Undaunted, I decided I would make up for my loss in speed with driving skill. None of the other kids on the course had been driving machines as long as I had. I was sure of that. One by one, I began to pass other cars on the corners, and then held them off on the straight-aways. In the fourth lap, over the roar of engines I heard, "Get outta my way!"

I glanced over my shoulder, and there was little Shirley, in *Blue* Number 33! She had a look on her face that I had never seen before.

Again she yelled, "Get outta my way!"

Yeah, right, there was no way she was going to get around ME! I held her off at every corner, and cut her off on the straight-aways. The man in charge waved the white flag. One lap to go. On the third corner, Shirley slid under me, and bumped me out of the way as I attempted to cut her off. She finished a good ten feet in front of me.

She had that typical "Shirley Smirk" as she got out of the car. "I think I like Go Karts," she said, as she turned and strode to her adoring parents.

Normally, I would have thought of a way to make her life miserable for the next week, but now, I had more important things on my mind.

"Dad," I said, as we left the fair. "I think I found something almost as fast as a sports car."

"You mean, like Go Karts?" he said, with a grin.

"Yes," I said. "I think we could build one with

stuff we have around the farm."

"I think you are right," he said, leaving it at that.

Wanting to verify what I thought I had just heard, I asked, "Do you mean we can build a Go Kart?"

"Absolutely!" he said. "As long as it is within reason and prudence."

Those words again!

"Yippee! We're going to build a Go Kart!" Shirley squealed. She had been listening around the corner.

"What do you mean, 'we?'" I said, as my joy turned to anger. I glared at Shirley. She snarled her lips and glared back. I pressed my advantage. "Girls don't drive Go Karts."

"Well, this one will," Mom said, jumping into the fray. "And not only that, but this will be a two-seater, so Shirley can ride with you."

I turned to my dad for support, but he just shrugged, gave me a sheepish look, and walked away. I had momentarily forgotten who was in charge.

Great, I thought, as we walked to the car. I will be the only kid in Weldon Valley with a 'sissy cart.'

My anger soon subsided, and by the next morning, I had drawings for a two-seat Go Kart. After a few changes, and some engineering by Dad, we had the design complete.

Construction began that very night. We used angle irons from an old bed for the frame, chain links from a beet harvester for steering linkage, and four hard rubber tires from a corn cultivator for wheels. A four horse-power gasoline motor provided the power. We took the pulleys from an old washing machine and made a reduction system from the motor to the wheels. I welded an old steering wheel in place. And, oh, yes, it had one wide seat that could accommodate two, if *absolutely* necessary.

It took two weeks of spare time, but the result was a masterpiece. We painted it with red tractor paint, and it gleamed like an Indianapolis race car.

The whole family was there for its maiden trip around the barnyard. I hopped in, and Dad started it. It was a noisy, smoky contraption. All of our animals, from milk cows to Shirley's beloved pet sheep, lined the corral fences to see what was going on.

I engaged the idler lever and was off with a lurch. It took some getting used to, but it was FUN, and best of all, it was FAST! After a few laps around the barnyard, Dad took it for a spin. True to form, he came back and made a number of changes.

Meanwhile, Shirley asked every five minutes, "Can I drive now? Can I drive, please? Is it my turn yet?"

Finally, I said she could go, but only if she took a ride with me first.

She grudgingly accepted and I proceeded to show her where the gas lever and the brake pedal were located. I slid over and let her try.

She was a crazy woman! She was all over the barnyard at full speed! I begged her to let me get off the thing. She accommodated, then she roared at full speed in a cloud of dust and smoke toward a group of unsuspecting chickens.

"Get outta my way!" she yelled, as she plowed a path through the cackling mob. "Get outta my way!"

she screamed, as she chased the yelping dog all the way to the main road. "Get outta my way!" she hollered, as she nipped her pet sheep in the rear end. "Get outta my way!" she intoned, as she headed straight toward me, and the picket fence.

Yeah, right, Sis, just turn the wheel and finish terrorizing the rest of the barn yard!

"Get outta my way," she said, with sheer terror in her eyes.

'Okay, real funny, Shirley,' I thought to myself, 'now quit joking around.' And then I saw it. She was holding the steering wheel, but it wasn't attached to anything! One of my welds must have come loose, and she was full speed, and out of control.

"Hit the brake! Hit the BRA...!"

I was diving over the picket fence when I heard her say, one last time, "Get outta my way!"

Those were the last words I heard on that fateful day in the late summer of '61. Oh, I did hear the scraping and the crunching. And the crashing. I heard that, too, as I was hung up on that picket fence in front of our farm house, in Weldon Valley, Colorado.

GRANDPA'S NEW TRACTOR

by Larry Wayne Miller

She was so-o-o-o-o beautiful! Breathtaking would be more accurate. As I was just an emerging nine-year-old, she was obviously way out of my league. She stood only five feet tall and yet she was strong, some would even say powerful. She was our pride and joy. She ...was... a tractor!

It was the summer of 1958, and at nine years old, I had never been this close to a brand-new tractor. The most intriguing fact was that this was a *little* tractor. It was my size. It was made for small jobs, like cultivating, or taking corn wagons from one place to another. It had a four-speed transmission, with a two-speed rear end. That meant it could go very, very slow-or up to 18 mph, which is fast for a tractor. For me, it was love at first sight!

It is a mystery to me why people identify cars, ships, and other mechanical objects as "she." Perhaps it is a feeling most closely associated with a "first love." In any case, the lady in question was a 1958 Ford tractor.

On our farms in Weldon Valley, Colorado, new equipment was always hard to come by. It was purchased only after careful investigation and proof of the need for it. So you can imagine my surprise when Grandpa granted me, a nine-year-old, my request to drive the brand new tractor home from the field back to the farm yard.

My father's father was the patriarch of the family. Although we held him in great esteem, we also trembled at his displeasure. An errant action could end up with a severe and immediate verbal reprimand. He believed his sons and grandsons should be hard workers, free from complaining or whimpering. They should be able to follow orders without having them repeated, and young men should work as hard and as long as their fathers, or grandfathers, in this case. Grandpa was tough but fair, and we all worked hard to make him proud of us.

Although I had been driving a tractor since I was seven, this was my greatest honor to date. I mounted the gray steed under the incredulous gaze of my younger cousins and listened to the instructions given, just once, as to its operation. I slowly let out the clutch and pointed it down the dirt road toward home.

I was cautious at first. I concentrated on keeping it exactly in the middle of the lane. When it came time to shift to the next gear I pushed in the clutch with my left foot and tried to shift. After some grinding I got it in place and let out the clutch. The tractor jumped, sputtered, and died. I had accidentally jumped two gears. With all of the blood rushing to my face, I started the whole process over. This time I was able to do everything in the proper order. I never looked back. In my few years, I had already learned what was expected: "Finish the task that is given, no matter what it takes." With that in mind, I shifted the two-speed rear end. I was beginning to fly.

When I was over the hill and out of sight I threw caution to the wind. The further I went, the bolder I became. My speed and courage increased with each passing fence post. Now I pushed it to full speed as a large cloud of prairie dust rose behind me in a fan-tail marking my progress.

I became curious about how far I had out-distanced the rest of the family, so I stood up and turned around in my seat to look. Thus, I broke the first rule I ever learned about driving a tractor!

As I turned, my steering arm pulled the tractor toward a brand-new three-wire barbed wire fence. I heard it before I saw it. The snap of splintering post and zinging wire brought me to a full awareness that something was terribly wrong. I turned back around to see Grandpa's new tractor clipping off poles, one after another - clip, clip, clip! Barbed wire threatened to encase me in a cocoon of steely death from head to toe.

Somehow, I brought Grandpa's pride and joy to a stop and turned off the engine. The silence was deafening. The birds weren't singing. The cows just stood there, jaws agape. The tractor was completely surrounded with barbed wire, which was still connected to the posts.

My first thought was of how I had earned Grandpa's wrath. My life was worth very little to me at that time. I could not look to see if he was coming. I could not turn without sharp steel barbs stinging me back into the gravity of the situation. My goose was cooked! I was in big, B-I-G, **big** trouble.

I waited for what seemed an eternity, until I heard the whine of an old Chevy truck speeding to the scene of the crime. My father jumped out before it had slid to a stop. Fear and worry were written on his face like I had never seen before. But his eyes did not concern me, nor did they concern those others who rushed to help. It was the person they turned to see coming along that I was concerned about.

Suddenly, I felt *his* presence. I knew *he* was there. I wanted to cry, but I could not allow myself to. I wanted to run away, but I couldn't move. More than anything, I wanted to just die. To my nine-year-old brain, death would be easier than life as a disappointment to my grandfather.

Time moved in slow motion. It was as if nature couldn't breathe. Finally, there he was – dark, granite eyes; a furrowed, weathered face; and brownish-gray hair combed to the side. I thought I knew what to expect. I thought I knew exactly how Grandpa would react. But as long as I live, I will never forget his words. With compassion in his eyes he said, "Are you all right, boy?" What? No strong reprimand? No angry criticism?

I couldn't believe it! Relief filled every part of my trembling body, and silently, I felt tears coursing my cheeks. He had forgiven me! He had showed his love for me, with just five simple words. Slowly, my dad and grandpa freed me from the barbed wire. From that day forward, Grandpa never mentioned the incident. In one simple gesture, it was wiped away and forgotten, though I would never forget what I learned that day.

FLYING!

by Larry Wayne Miller

"Look, Dad, it's an old DC-3." My excitement was barely contained as I continued, "Look, it's got its landing gear down." Dad grudgingly snuck a peek towards the western Colorado sky while I pointed at the speck in the distance. Then we turned our attention to the corn rows passing slowly underneath the old Minneapolis 'Z' tractor.

Dad had spent the better part of the morning teaching me how to cultivate new corn. For my part, I had learned all I needed to know in the first twenty minutes and had spent the morning perched on the old yellow tractor's fender, talking non-stop to Dad about life and airplanes, which at that time were the same thing, for me.

"How do you know it has its wheels down?" Dad said, sneaking another peek at the dot in the sky.

"You can just see it," I replied, "Take a look."

Dad squinted into the sky again. "I can hardly see the plane, let alone the wheels."

He shook his head and grimaced a half smile. "I hope you can put a small amount of that enthusiasm into cultivating this furrow."

It had been like that since I had been old enough to ask Mom what that noisy thing in the sky was. I was eight years old, going to be nine in a few days, and I knew every type of plane I saw: how many passengers or how much cargo it would hold, what type of engines it had, and its range in nautical miles.

Another movement in the sky caught my attention, and I said, "Look, Dad, it's a Cessna 150, at 3 o'clock."

"No, it's not," he said, slightly irritated, "It's only 11 o'clock. A.M."

"No," I said with a laugh. "A pilot divides the sky into twelve equal parts like sections of a clock. Twelve o'clock is lined up with the nose of the airplane, or for us, with the nose of the tractor. That means 3 o'clock is over the right side of the tractor."

With that, I pointed past his face over the right side of the tractor, dislodging his cap in the process. He grabbed his cap, scrunched it on tight, and gave me a look as if to say, 'enough of this airplane stuff, okay?' Then he said, "Enough of this airplane stuff, okay? You are going to be driving this tractor alone in a few minutes and I want you to concentrate so you won't cover up corn."

Cultivating was probably the most tedious job on the farm. Sharp metal blades that were shaped like a "V" hung on an apparatus under the tractor. When operated properly, they cut through the roots of weeds, covered them with a thin layer of dirt, and formed a uniform ditch for the irrigation water to run down. All the while, the operator had to be careful not to cover or cut the tender corn shoots that were barely out of the ground. It took relentless, exacting concentration for twelve to fourteen hours a day.

The best cultivators were women. Their meticulous eye for detail and their ability to concentrate for long periods of time made them ideally suited for the job. Mom did her share of cultivating, and so did Grandma. This left the men free to do the more 'manly' jobs. The truth was most men were ill-suited or tempered to last through the long day of cultivating.

At the end of the row, Dad disengaged the clutch, slid out of the tractor seat, and stood on the tail bar while I got situated to drive. During the next half hour he taught me the little nuances it took to protect the fresh, green shoots of corn.

At last it was time to try it alone. A Minneapolis 'Z' tractor has a hand clutch which was never designed for an eight-year-old boy to engage. Dad showed me how to hold on to the steering wheel with both hands, lean back, and push the hand clutch in with my right foot. All worked as planned, and before I knew it, I had lowered the cultivator and was creeping down the field at all of one mile-per-hour. My technique was good, my concentration was good, but oh, this was so *boring*. And I was going to do this all summer?

I turned at the end of the row and headed back to where Dad was waiting. It had already taken me twenty minutes, but Dad was patiently leaning on the fender of our old blue 1949 Chevy pickup truck. I was happy to see him there. I had spent the last few years at his side on the farm, and did not relish the idea of spending so much of the day alone.

Suddenly a large dark shadow passed over me, followed by the most beautiful deep, throaty sound I had ever heard. It was a Wright Whirlwind radial engine. I looked up in time to see a vintage Stearman biplane pass a mere fifty feet overhead. It banked steeply to the right and landed on a dirt road that led to our house. It had been converted into a crop-duster. A pesticide tanker truck was waiting to refill it. I had seen them in the sky but never this close.

I looked to Dad and he was waving at me. I waved back and pointed to the airplane. He did not seem to notice and began waving with both arms. Then it hit me. The tractor was still going but it had been a long time since I had been driving. I grabbed the steering wheel and quickly got back into the correct row. I yanked back the hand clutch and sat there trembling while I watched Dad run full speed over the corn rows, straight at me.

I should have been scared. I should have been fearful for my life. But at that moment something caught me funny. It was Dad. I had never seen him run before. He looked to me like a buffalo in suspenders. His massive arms were a-churnin' and his red suspenders kept falling down. Dirt was flying everywhere. I couldn't help it. I started laughing until tears rolled down my face.

When he got to me, he was out of breath but still managed, "What?" The look on his face was totally exhausted exasperation. "What's so funny?" he repeated, a little more pointedly.

"I'm sorry, Dad, but you look so funny when you run."

His eyebrows lowered, his face got red, and he said, "Maybe you think that is funny." He was pointing at the disaster behind me. All humor left my body. "Son," he said, in a calmer tone. "That is our livelihood. That is what feeds us for the year. This airplane business has gotten way out of hand. You are almost nine years old and that is old enough to take some responsibility."

He put his hands on his hips and looked at me for a while. There was nothing I could say. Finally he broke the silence and said, "Grab those leather gloves out of the toolbox and help me."

During the next thirty minutes we carefully replanted 100 feet of baby corn. No words were said but I had learned my lesson. When we'd finished, Dad drove to the end of the road. "We might as well break for lunch."

The Stearman biplane was still on the side road. I could see the pilot leaning against the lower wing, eating a sandwich. I was vaguely aware that Dad had opened his lunch pack and was eating, but I couldn't eat. I couldn't move. There was a Stearman biplane a mere 300 feet away! I heard Dad click the snaps on his lunch pail.

"Are you done already?" I asked.

"No," he said. "I thought maybe we could finish over by the airplane."

A smile creased his face and I let out a "Yippee!" In no time I was asking the pilot a million questions about the airplane and what he did while flying it. Much too soon, he was ready to go. Dad and I drew back so he could start the engine.

The pilot pulled on a leather helmet, paused, and looked at me. "Would you like to sit in it?" he asked, with a smile.

"Would I ever!" I shouted, looking up at Dad for approval. He nodded and I carefully got up on the wing. The pilot lifted me into the open cockpit. I did not know whether to cry or scream. This was where I was born to be! There was a metal pole with the hand grip between my legs, and pedals on each side. There were dials and switches on the firewall, and somehow I knew what they all did. I told the pilot how they functioned and the basic laws of aerodynamics.

"Where did you learn so much about airplanes?" he quizzed.

"I don't know," I said, honestly.

Dad came up and said, "We've got to let this man get back to work." I hopped out. Dad and I watched as the heavily loaded plane roared down the dirt road and barely cleared some cottonwood trees.

Dad took me back to the tractor and asked me, before he left, "Can you do this now? No forgetting to drive because you're gazing at airplanes, right?" I nodded yes, trying to show as much courage as possible. He got in the truck, rolled down the window, and added with a grin, "If you have to look at airplanes, will you please stop the tractor first?" I waved and smiled as he drove out of sight.

He was back two hours later. I'd only had to stop the tractor three times. Day after day of monotonous cultivating had begun to take its toll on me. I was used to recess, trips to Fort Morgan for tractor parts, and long hours sitting on the fender of Dad's tractor, talking about life. I found that when I developed a feel for the tractor I could detach part of my brain for more important stuff like daydreaming. And, oh, what a rich fantasy life I had. Slowly, I began to develop a plan.

The owner of the farm we rented had a brother named Virgil Mylander. His farm was kitty-corner from ours. He loved airplanes, too. In fact, he had built a Cessna 172 from the parts of a number of wrecked Cessna's that he had collected over the years. The unused parts were in the top of our barn.

I had spent many an evening going through the pieces, seeing how they worked and how they were made. So now, I started to lay out the airplane parts. There was half a wing, part of a fuselage, and most of a bent tail section. They looked to me like a dismembered tin bird as they sat softly on the hay and straw in the loft.

That evening, after supper, I dragged Dad, lantern in hand, to the barn to present my idea. I had him sit on a bale of hay while I raised the lantern high. He looked at the scene before him, then to me, then back to the mangled airplane parts. I could not stand it any longer and said, "Well, what do you think?"

He looked at me with eyes that said, 'I know I should get this, but I don't have a clue what's going on here.'

Finally he did say, "What are you talking about?"

"It's an airplane, Dad," I replied. "I think I can take these parts and make an airplane."

His eyebrows arched as he said, "Oh." He cocked his head to one side, looked at me and said,   "What are you going to use for wheels?"

"We have two old matching wheelbarrow tires in the garage. I'm sure of it."

"How about an engine?" he continued.

"I thought maybe we could use the extra swather engine," I said. Never mind that it weighed too much, or didn't run too well, and it was still attached to the swather.

He could have blown me out of the water right then and there, but he didn't. He just said, "All right, you draw up some plans and show me exactly how it can be done and I will ask Virgil if we can try." We – he said – we! When I got back to the house I got out my Big Chief tablet and began drawing plans.

As Mom tucked me into bed that night, she said, "You're going to be nine years old on Saturday."

I was lost in thought but managed to say, "Yes, Mom, I know."

"We are going to have a party at Grandma Miller's that evening," she continued. I didn't answer. I only looked at the ceiling.

Finally, Mom said, "Larry, what's wrong?"

Until that moment, I had not realized anything was wrong, but now I had to tell her.

"Mom, I can't stop thinking about airplanes. Every spare minute my brain is full of stuff about flying. Is there something wrong with me?"

She smiled and tucked the quilt a little tighter around my shoulders. "No, there is nothing wrong with you. In fact, you are lucky to have something that you are passionate about at your age. There will be other passions in your life, so just enjoy this one while you have it." I fell asleep, imagining I was putting together an airplane with the pieces in the barn.

Over the next two days, I drew all my plans for putting the airplane together. Dad even helped me rig the two wheelbarrow tires together. But more and more it became apparent to even my young mind that the project was never going to fly. There was a reason all these parts had been sitting unused in the barn for years.

By Friday evening I was feeling pretty blue. After supper I sat on the front porch to watch the sunset over the Rocky Mountains. When Mom had finished the dishes, she came out and sat beside me.

"You will be nine years old tomorrow," she said cheerfully.

"One more year and no closer to an airplane," I said, feeling sorry for myself.

"Well, maybe this will help you," she said, as she put her hand in her apron pocket. Then she pulled out the most beautiful balsa wood airplane I had ever seen. It even had a propeller with a rubber band!

"Wow! Thanks, Mom," I said, giving her a big

hug.

"Thank your dad," she said. "He sent me to Fort Morgan and said not to come back until I found the best plane in town."

I put it together and watched it soar on the wind until the sun was long gone and the yard light followed its path around the barnyard. Dad and Mom sat on the porch sipping coffee. My six-year-old sister, Shirley, acted as my airplane caddy.

The next morning Mom fixed my favorite breakfast, buttermilk pancakes with peanut butter and real maple syrup on top. I still had to cultivate corn, but I would get off early in time for the party. I did not mind driving the tractor that morning. It was a perfect early summer day. Everything was blooming and there were lots of planes in the sky.

At lunch I had a special treat. Dad joined me, as usual, but Mom and Shirley came in our old '49 DeSoto, also. They had lunch packed for all of us. We sat under a cottonwood tree on an old army blanket, covered by a red and white gingham tablecloth.

When we finished, Mom pulled out a birthday cake shaped like an airplane. The propeller was made of birthday candles!

"Wow! That is so cool! Thanks, Mom," I said.

"Thank your sister," she said. "It was her idea and she did all the work."

I looked at Shirley in amazement and gave her a big hug.

As we finished the last bite, I heard the drone of an airplane in the distance. But I did not notice much. I was enjoying the moment.

"Look, Larry," Dad said. "I think that is a Cessna 172."

I looked up at the sky and then at Dad. It was a Cessna 172. But how would he know?

"I think that model has a Lycoming engine and carries four passengers," he continued. "It can fly nearly 600 miles with large fuel tanks."

I was trying to figure out how he knew all this Cessna stuff as the airplane swooped low and landed on the road next to our field.

"Let's go take a look," Dad said. I was getting suspicious, now.

The Cessna was still idling as the pilot opened the passenger door. He smiled and held the door open against the rushing wind, as Dad yelled over the roar of the engine. "Larry, I would like to introduce you to Virgil Milander. He owns the airplane parts in our barn."

I could not say a word as I reached out my hand and shook the hand of a real live pilot.

"I hear you like airplanes," Virgil yelled out of the cockpit. "Why don't you hop in and we'll take it for a spin?"

Immediately all the blood left my upper body. I thought I was going to pass out, but there was no time. Dad picked me up and put on my seat belt real tight. Before he closed the door, I yelled out to him, "Dad, thank you for the best gift of my life."

"Don't thank me. Your mom said, 'Go to Virgil, and don't come back until we get that boy in the air.' "

4/4 TIME

by Larry Wayne Miller

I was eight years old and it was late August, 1957. I was sitting on the very top of the rusty cab of our old Chevy farm truck. My shoes and socks were sitting beside me. My pants were rolled up carefully and my legs were up to their knees in three tons of last year's feed corn. My father was scooping it into a 2' x 2' grain door in the side of our big red barn.

"How do you do it, Dad?" I asked.

He didn't pause or look up from his rhythmic scooping. "How do I do what, Son?"

"How do you shovel and shovel and shovel all

day long and never stop?"

Still he didn't stop, but he did chuckle at my childish exaggeration. "Even *I* couldn't do this all day long." He paused, and then continued. "But you have to realize I have been doing this since I was your age."

I was intrigued. I had been driving a cultivating tractor for over a year and I had driven a truck just like this one during harvest, but still I couldn't imagine doing that much work, all at one time, day after day.

"Would you show me?"

"Sure," he said. "Let's start right now."

One of Dad's mottos - one that continually got him in trouble with Mom - was, 'If you are old enough to ask, then you are old enough to learn,' and that applied to *everything.*

I started to get up from my perch. He said, "No, you stay there. You need to learn first things first." He finally stopped shoveling, stuck the scoop deep into the corn and leaned on it. Sweat was dripping off his face and into the corn. His shirt and coveralls were totally soaked. At 7 o'clock at night it was still over 100° on the Colorado plains. He must have been terribly uncomfortable. And yet, he had a big warm smile for me.

"Did you notice anything about the way I shoveled?" he asked.

"You never stop," I said.

"More than that," he urged.

"You never stop sweating," I teased.

He was not amused. "Now come on, Larry, you can do better than that. What is the most obvious thing I do?"

I thought for a while. "Your speed is exactly the same, all the time."

"That's it!" he exclaimed. "You hit the corn right on the kernel."

I grinned at his silly joke. He chuckled and resumed his scooping.

"You're taking piano lessons." It wasn't a question. It was just a statement.

"Yes, I am. It's really boring." One of the refreshing truisms of being raised on a farm in northeastern Colorado in the 1950's was that everyone spoke their minds. That is, they didn't try to sugarcoat what they thought. They felt it was a waste of time. I didn't hear about political correctness until I got to college. (There I learned that political correctness was meant for politicians, used car salesmen, and preachers.)

Dad glanced up, his eyebrows raised as he drove the scoop deep into the corn. "You realize who your teacher is, don't you?"

"Yes," I said. "Grandma Miller."

"And, she's my mother," he countered.

"I know, but, Dad," I whined. "I sit there all day and do the same thing over and over and over. I never get anywhere."

"In case you hadn't noticed, that is what I am doing right now."

"Yes, but Dad, you *are* getting somewhere," I lamented.

"Could your attitude have anything to do with the fact that you never practice between lessons?"

I looked down at the corn and drove my feet

further into its cool pebbly roughness. I hated piano lessons. They took me away from the farm, the animals, the machinery, the men, and all that was outdoors.

"You don't understand, Dad, it's about more than the lessons."

"I do understand, Son. I took piano lessons at your age. From the very same woman."

"You did?"

"Yes, I did. And she was a lot harder on me than she will ever be on you." I doubted that, but did not dare say so.

Dad decided to take a different tack. "What is the third thing on a line of music?"

"Huh? What does music have to do with scooping corn?"

"Just answer me."

I looked up at the big red barn and thought about it. "First is the staff… Then there is the key signature… And the third thing is…is… the time signature."

"And what is the time signature that you use the most?" Dad asked.

Without hesitation, I chirped, "4/4 time."

"You've been singing since you could talk," he said. "So now, with your new superior knowledge, which was gleaned from your boring grandmother, what is the time signature for almost all of the hymns we sing at church?"

Now he had my interest. "4/4 time!"

"Now, Larry, don't say a word. Don't even think. Just listen and feel, and when you figure it out, then you can join in."

I was confused, but I obeyed. Then I watched Dad dig the scoop deep into the corn and with one swinging motion throw it into the corn bin in the barn without losing one single kernel. Scoop and throw. Scoop and throw. Scoop and throw and scoop and throw and....

Then it hit me! With unveiled emotion I began to sing the chorus of my favorite song, an old favorite by Elton Roth:

"In my heart there rings a melody,
There rings a melody,
With heaven's harmony."
Scoop and throw and scoop and throw and,
"In my heart there rings a melody,
There rings of melody of love."
Scoop and throw and scoop and throw and...

He looked up, and without missing a beat, said, "Now, sing the first verse."
"I have a song that Jesus gave me,
It was sent from heaven above,"
Scoop and throw...
"There never was a sweeter Melody,
'Tis the melody of Love!"

Dad joined in on the chorus, and during the next half hour we sang dozens of old hymns. My bare feet were hanging loose in space, with a cool Colorado breeze tickling my ankles, as we finished the load of grain.
"Sunshine, sunshine, in my soul today..."

After I put on my shoes and socks Dad handed me the shovel. The handle was polished to an almost mahogany sheen by its constant use and tender care. I took it with awe. Dad showed me where the center of balance was and helped me put my left hand there.

Then he said, "Son, sweep all of the kernels to the back of the box and then shovel the rest into the barn. Don't miss one single kernel. I have some work to do in the barn to get ready for tomorrow morning's milking. Finish it up and then we'll have a bowl of ice cream in the house."

Dad was famous for always wanting a bowl of ice cream at the end of a very long hot day, and I was never one to say 'no' to one myself.

During the next twenty minutes I swept and scooped and swept and scooped. It was difficult to get all of the corn out of the small cracks near the sideboard and the end gate, but I did it, and was quite proud of myself. Dad helped me get out of the back of the truck and then pulled it forward a few feet. He stood there looking at the side of the barn.

I said, "Time to go get some ice cream, right?"

He said, "Take a good look at the barn and tell me what you see."

I saw a big red barn reflecting a big red Colorado sun as it dipped behind the Rocky Mountains.

"I see a job well done," I said, with a certain pride.

"I see a lot of corn sitting on a canvas tarp below the grain door."

Oops! I looked with dismay. There *was* a pile of grain sitting on the tarp next to the concrete wall. It appeared to be about as large as the amount I thought I had scooped into the barn.

"We'll finish it together today, Son, and *then* we'll have ice cream," Dad said, with a wink. "But next time, you'll do it by yourself."

*　　　　　*　　　　　*

Then I was ten, and it was the summer of 1959. Once again, we were scooping corn into the 2'x2' grain door in the big red barn. The major difference was that this corn was 'rolled corn.' Cows are notoriously inept at being able to process their food. So in order to keep more of the nutrients inside of the cow, farmers would flatten the grain by running it through two large rollers. This left the soft inside of the grain more palatable to the digestion process.

The other difference was that, more and more, Dad was allowing me to finish up scooping the truck. I still had a lot of cleanup to do, but I was learning. He showed me that by twisting the scoop slightly as I threw the corn into the grain bin, the corn seemed to stay together in a stream longer. He called it rifling. He said it was like the rifling in the barrel of a gun that turns the bullet as it travels toward the target, thus making it more accurate. I could see that the grain seemed to stay together more as it went through the grain door when I gave it that twist.

He also showed me how to take care of the big scoop. He showed me how to file out nicks and burrs on the end of the shovel so that it would enter the corn more smoothly and efficiently. He showed me how to sand and oil the handle so that slivers and splits wouldn't occur. He admonished me to never leave a shovel leaning against anything. "The bottom will begin to rust and pit, even if you can't see it."

Then, he imparted to me the wisdom he would remind me of more than a thousand times before I was twelve years old: "Take care of your tools and they will take care of you."

Finally, after all this, he smiled and said, "I have a surprise for you."

He went into the barn. Soon he produced, from just inside the big barn door, a scoop shovel. Just like his, but a bit smaller.

"Son, this belonged to your great-grandfather. It was brought to Colorado from Iowa by my father. I know you will take care of it, just as three generations of Miller men who came before you have."

I took it in my hands. Even though it was smaller, it seemed substantial. The main difference was that the handle was wood all the way up. The only metal were the scoop itself and the bolt that went through the wooden handle to hold it together.

"I will leave it to you to file it, sand it, and oil it yourself." As he put his foot on the big rear tire of the truck and proceeded into the box he said, "Today, we work together. We'll unload this truck side-by-side."

Never had there been words uttered to me that meant so much and would last so long.

We worked as two men together. He scooped and then I scooped. He sang and I sang with him. He sweated, and so did I. Every one hundred scoops we traded sides to rest our over-taxed muscles. It was very difficult to mirror the scooping motion with appendages that had not yet learned to reverse the motion.

Then we started singing. We finished twenty minutes later, by singing a rousing rendition of -

"Wonderful grace of Jesus,
Greater than all my sin."
Scoop and throw
"How shall my tongue describe it,
Where shall my praise begin?"
Scoop and throw

I had a hard time keeping up with Dad but I wasn't about to let him down. We ended with a big grand finale.

"Wonderful the matchless grace of Jesus,
Deeper than the mighty rolling sea,
Higher than a mountain,
Sparkling like a fountain.
All sufficient grace for even me.
Broader than the scope of my transgressions,
Greater far then all my sin and shame,
Oh, <u>magnify</u> the precious name of Jesus.
Praise his name!"

It was that amazing song by Haldor Lilliness. The cows were impressed. They moo-ed their ovation. When we pulled the truck away from the barn, there was less than a gallon of corn on the tarp. Dad looked at me, smiled and said, "I've got this, Son."

But I wasn't leaving now that we were only moments from being finished. He swept and I folded the canvas tarp. Life was never better than that summer day in 1959.

*   *   *

Then I was twelve, and it was 1961. Dad and I had been working side by side for four years. Not only were we shoveling grain side-by-side, but we'd been cleaning out irrigation ditches where they lead from the main ditch to the corn. It was backbreaking work, but again I got to work with my dad with an irrigation shovel, and occasionally a hand pick, instead of a scoop shovel. Sometimes the dirt was as hard as concrete with a heavy clay content. I learned that Dad had done exactly the same job with his father twenty-two years earlier. We talked as we worked, but under the admonition that my father constantly gave to me, 'Talk all you want, as long as it doesn't interfere with your work.' Hour after hour, day after day, we scooped the Colorado prairie.

By this point in my life, I could work side-by-side with any man, and carry my own weight, all day long and all night, if that was what it took. It was what was expected of a Miller man, and I carried that knowledge as a badge of not-so-humble pride.

One day as we finished I began to clean, file, and oil the two shovels. They didn't really need it, but I wanted to show off for my dad.

"You're as good as any man I've ever worked with," said Dad, "But remember this, let your work speak for itself. Let others praise you. Don't draw attention to yourself." These were lessons I never forgot and have shaped me to this very day.

*   *   *

Then I was sixteen. Dad no longer had dominion over the scene. He was off somewhere else, doing something important - another story for another time. Now I was the mentor. My younger cousin Cliff and I were scooping corn into an auger that took kernels to a hole in the top of a metal silo. It didn't take long for us to get a rhythm going. Cliff was a much faster learner than I had been. It was a big job and after a while we began to lag. A few times our scoop shovels clicked against each other, spilling the precious corn and ruining our rhythm. That would not do!

"Gotta teach you something my dad taught me, back a few years," I said, stopping for a breather. Soon I began to hum, and we got back to work. The songs were the only songs I really knew. They were, of course, church songs. All of them were in 4/4 time. Cliff wasn't anywhere near as demonstrative as I was, so he was content to listen to my humming. But he got the point. He just listened and matched his rhythm to the song. When at last we finished, we were both hot, sweaty, and completely content. A job well done, side by side, no words spoken - only the language of work hanging in the air.

*   *   *

Today, I'm sixty five. I'm scooping snow out of the driveway. I have been at it for over an hour. I have a rhythm going. I don't slow down. I don't stop. I just scoop and throw and scoop and throw and... then I realize that I am singing. I have been all along. Suddenly, it all washes over me...the memories, the emotion....

Dad has been gone for eighteen years, but it seems just like yesterday. His grin. The smell of corn and sweat and soil. I start to hear something from long, long ago.... A song...

"When we all get to heaven,
What a day of rejoicing that will be!
Scoop and throw
When we all see Jesus,
We'll sing and shout the victory!"
Scoop and throw, scoop and throw.

HUMM BATTA BATTA

by Larry Wayne Miller

"Humm Batta Batta, swingggg, batta, batta! Put that ball right in there. Put that ol' ball right in this big ol' glove. Hummm batta batta. Come on pitcher put it right there. Let's go pitcher. Let's get that ball zippin' in there!"

The catcher was unusually vocal today. But as I spit in my glove, adjusted my cap, and felt for the seams in the ball, I was grateful for the practice. My first high school game was just days away. I wasn't pitcher for the team, but I badly needed to work on arm strength.

"Humm batta batta. Swingg batta batta." The catcher stood up and with hands on hips said, "Hey, pitcher! What is the problem?"

The problem was that the catcher was wearing a blue cotton dress and a white ruffled apron. The problem was that she was my mother! It would have been embarrassing if this hadn't been our farm-yard, with the closest neighbor a quarter mile away.

"Are you going to pitch or not? I have a meatloaf that will be done in fifteen minutes."

Meatloaf! I loved meatloaf! Next to peanut butter on macaroni and cheese, it was the best food in the world. I wound up and threw the hardball toward Mom and the catcher's mitt the school had let me borrow for practice. I had never played real baseball before. In Weldona, Colorado, all twelve grades were in the same building. I was recruited in the eighth grade and was delighted to get a chance to start, even though it was because no one else wanted to play catcher. All the men were spring plowing, so Mom took a little time each evening helping me get used to the small hardball.

Whack! Mom's eyes widened a little as the ball slapped the catcher's mitt. She straightened up and threw the ball with enough zip that it stung my hand when I caught it. I thought I detected a slight smirk spread across her face.

"Hey, Mom, where did you learn to throw like that?" I asked while returning the ball and trying to shake the stinging from my hand.

"I played a lot of sports in school and with my

brothers…." Whack! The ball stung me again.

I had to smile to myself. In all of my growing up, I'd never gotten the best of Mom. She was always surprising me. Although Dad had taught me a lot about being a man, Mom had been the one who taught me the subtleties it took to survive in a changing world. My earliest memories were of Mom teaching me to chew with my mouth closed, elbows off the table, napkin in my lap. To never, ever interrupt the conversation. To eat some of everything (especially the green stuff.) What to do with all the different silverware.

By the time I was four, I was opening doors for all the ladies, and waiting for them to be seated before seating myself. Turning five found me graduating to car doors, and I was also changing my own sheets and making my own bed. It was then that I started bathing more than twice a week. At six I started making some of my own meals and polishing my shoes. Regular kitchen chores had to be done before working on the farm chores. At age eight I learned how to wash and iron my own clothes, not mixing colors. Nine found me being driven to swimming lessons twice a week in spite of the fact that there were chores to be done, and at night, I learned to mend clothes while I watched Jackie Gleason on "The Honeymooners."

Grooming and personal hygiene were tackled next. Deodorant, Vitalis, and shaving cream were new on my shelf. I started shaving when I was ten. All the questions about girls came at eleven. I had to read a whole bunch of books about the changes in the body and to learn how life begins. At twelve, I got to sit at the adult table at family reunions. I learned how to listen first and speak intelligently. But all during this time there was music.

My earliest memories are of coming into the house and hearing classical music being played on the Philco. Mom would buy used records and "fill in the gaps" with my first taste of culture. I would wake up listening to Tennessee Ernie Ford or a gospel quartet, and go to sleep listening to Beethoven's "Moonlight Sonata." But, I digress.

"Well, that's it, Son. My meatloaf is calling." With that, she straightened her apron, handed me the mitt, and strode into the house. I stayed for a few minutes to practice my throw to second base. It was the weakest part of my game. I was wild. Sometimes I couldn't even get it back to the pitcher. The shortstop might have to chase it down. Or the outfielder.

I picked the place on the big barn door and threw for the next ten minutes. I was either ten feet high, or ten feet wide. Once I almost took out a window twenty feet away.

The sun was setting and I had to do a few more chores before supper. As I fed the pigs, I thought about the big game coming up. I wasn't ready, I knew that much. It would take a miracle. I entered the lean-to porch, and as the screen door slammed behind me I heard Mom call out from the kitchen, "You don't have to get it all the way to second base in the air. Let it bounce once."

Right. That showed how much she knew about baseball. I would be laughed right out of the school. As if she could hear my thoughts she said, "Johnny

Bench had to start somewhere." Johnny Bench! He was every catcher's hero. But I bet he could get the ball to second base by the time he was four.

The next few days went quickly. I only made it to practice once. The day before the game I had to plow at my Uncle Roy's. During the spring, most of us boys only attended class about half the time. When the weather broke we had to get the crops planted. So, there were very few practices where there were nine of us to play. A lot of the teachers would come out and play with us. But when the big day came, I awoke with the realization that I had never played a full game of baseball in my life.

It was a bright, beautiful spring day. Temperatures were in the 70's and there was no wind, which is unusual for the plains of Colorado. The minute the last school bell rang, all eleven of us baseball players (which was just about every boy in school) got dressed and headed for the pasture. That's right. The pasture! The school didn't have enough land for a field, so one of the local farmers loaned the space. He still ran cows on the land, so on game day all the players and parents herded the cows into an adjoining field and closed the gate.

There were no bleachers, so fans lined two sides of the field with their cars, old trucks, and a few tractors with hay wagons. A lot of people brought lunches, soda pop, and big blankets.

Mom leaned up against the hood of our old Chrysler with a few of the other kids' mothers. While they were settling in, we took out scoop shovels and cleared the rest of the cow messes out of the infield, and sprinkled dirt over the rest. The other hindrance to playing was the corn field in right field. Twenty feet past first base was the remnants of last year's crop – naked stalks still high with deep furrows running the whole length of the field.

We had to get a volunteer to play Right Fielder with those conditions. No one in their right mind would play that position. We found just the guy. Ralphie. A recent transfer to Weldona High, he was glad to have the chance to play. He stood six foot one when he didn't slump, and he was blind as a bat without his glasses. But since Philip, the best pitcher in the league, was our pitcher today, there would not be much action out there. No one hit to right field on Philip.

Just as we finished scooping up the messes in the infield, the bus from Prairie High School drove up. They were an even smaller school than Weldona, but they had new uniforms. We were still wearing the wool outfits my dad had worn when he played in high school. I couldn't wear the pants, as they gave me a rash, so I was wearing jeans. That was why the other team promptly protested. The umpire, a local wheat farmer, said, "Yah, yah, we came to play ball, so let's play. Get on with the game!"

For some strange reason, we were put up to bat first. I went ahead and put on my catcher's stuff. I was at the bottom of the order so they wouldn't get to me this inning. It was all so fast! Five up. Three down. We even scored a run!

I was still adjusting my equipment when I heard, "Miller, let's go. Warm up the pitcher." I was in a fog.

Soon, the warm-up pitches done, it was time to do the customary practice throw to second base. By prior arrangement, I threw to the pitcher so they wouldn't know how weak my arm was. Before I knew it, the inning was over. Three up. Three down. Philip could throw a 90 mile per hour fast ball, but he was wild. Most of the batters struck out, trying to defend themselves from the errant pitches. Over the next three innings, we scored two more runs. The score was 3-0. Then came the fifth inning.

Philip was getting tired. Someone got a single off him. As I squatted into position, I realized no one was out there and there was an eager runner on first base. He didn't know I couldn't throw, but he would soon find out. On the first pitch, he took off to steal second base. I threw the ball with all my might. Clear over second base, clear into centerfield. The runner went to third. On the next pitch, the batter bunted up the third base line. It was a race to see who would get to home base first, the catcher (that was me) or the runner from third. He won the race. Running over me in the process.

As I lay in a pile of dust and sand burrs, I could hear the team yelling "Throw to second! Get up and throw!" I couldn't move. Finally Philip arrived just as the runner got to third. We called time-out and he had a *chat* with me. Time in. More of the same. When the inning was over, they had scored four runs and I had thrown to the outfield three times. I'm sure the coach would have taken me out if he had a substitute for me.

As we moved into the eighth inning we were still down only 4-3. I was at bat with two men on and two outs. I had struck out every time so far. The count was 3 and 2. Then I lofted what should have been an easy out to right field. The fielder fell down in the corn rows and didn't find the ball until I was standing at second base.

I looked over at Mom. She gave me a big smile. We were ahead 5 to 4 and that is how it stayed because our next hitter struck out. In the bottom of the eighth, the coach put in a new pitcher, Ed. Ed was about six feet tall and looked like Hoss Cartright in baseball pants. He threw hard but his best pitch was a wicked change-up.

The first two batters went down with a strike-out and a grounder to the short stop. The third hitter hit a triple and stood on third base with the tie-ing run. The next hitter popped the ball straight up. Up into the blinding sun. I looked down and blinked.

Everyone was screaming and pointing. I looked up and finally saw the ball just ten feet off the ground. I dove full out and caught it just inches off the ground.

The crowd cheered and then came a collective "oooh" and then an "ohh, yuk!" I had dived flat out into a fresh cow pie! I could feel a warm aromatic wetness pervade every inch of my chest and neck. I wanted to crawl in a hole.

The inning was over, but no one came to congratulate me. Ralphie brought corn stalks from right field to clean me up as much as he could. He was the only one who would get near me. Mom brought an old towel from the car, poured some water on it, and wiped me off as much as she could.

During the top half of the ninth inning, the coach

had me coach first base. Their first baseman growled at me, "Back up!" By now my wool shirt was starting to itch and chafe, and of course, to stink to high heaven. To my relief the top of the ninth ended quickly but we didn't score any runs.

The bottom of the ninth started out badly. The first batter singled, then stole second base. By now all the outfielders were getting smart. When they knew I was getting ready to throw, they all covered somewhere near second base. The next hitter got a single to right, but, for some reason, the lead runner held up at third base. Men on first and third, and no outs. Arghh! My heart sank at the prospect of having to throw to second again. Then from the crowd I heard the voice of my mother crying, "Remember Johnny Bench!"

I stood up and called time out, and turned to my mother. She smiled and I knew. Then turning, I said, "Let's do it."

We were going to lose this game unless a miracle happened. It did. It was Ralphie. Ralphie the Miracle. The next hitter did something that had not been done all day. He hit a towering ball to right field. To the corn field. To Ralphie. Ralphie stood transfixed while the ball reached its apex, shielding his eyes from the sun with his glove, looking like a spectator. At last he spotted the ball and started for it. On the third step he fell full face into a corn row. The runners at third and first started running, knowing that Ralphie didn't have a chance of catching the ball.

The crowd was screaming, "Get up! Get up!" He did, but his glasses were gone. Oh, no! He squinted into the sun and with one huge leap, caught the ball. HE CAUGHT THE BALL! RALPHIE, THROW IT! Realizing their mistake, the runners backtracked and tagged up. Then started off again.

Right then the second miracle happened. Ralphie threw the ball, with no glasses, standing in uneven corn rows, straight as an arrow – at me. The runner was coming fast, and I set myself for the collision and waited for the ball. It got there a split second ahead of the runner. But this time I wasn't taking it. I shielded the ball and charged straight over the runner.

In a cloud of dust and sweat, an old Colorado wheat farmer raised his thumb and called, "You'rrrre Out." I didn't have time to celebrate. The man on first decided to steal second. As I wound up to throw from my knees, I could hear the second baseman yelling, "No! No!" Too late, I threw a perfect bounce straight into his glove and with a sweep of that glove, the game was over! A triple play! The crowd went wild.

As I took off my protective gear, I got a lot of pats on the back. Feeling like an old tired victorious warrior, I walked my mom to our Chrysler. Instinctively, I opened the door for her and waited until she tucked her skirt in. She looked at me and said, "I'm proud of you, Son, not just for winning the ball game but for not giving up!" With a big smile originating deep in my chest, I closed the door and waved goodbye.

In that moment, I realized my father had taught me all I knew about becoming a man, but my mom had taught me how to be a gentleman.

THANKSGIVING A LA PEANUT BUTTER

by Larry Wayne Miller

The worst part about waiting is…the waiting. And waiting seemed to be most of what I had been doing for the last two weeks in November of 1963.

The harvest was almost complete on the Colorado plain, in Weldona, Colorado. So with a little extra time to prepare, Mom had invited our new pastor and his family for Thanksgiving dinner. It was a big deal around our home. We scrubbed the house from top to bottom, dusted everything in sight, and beat the braided rugs. Mom dug up some real china, hid the Melmac dishes, and brought out an intricate lace table cloth. The whole family had focused on this one day, this one meal. Dad had even parked all of the machinery in one neat long row along the cottonwood trees.

As a fourteen year old, my motivations were more basic. The new pastor had a thirteen year old daughter. From the moment I laid eyes on her, I was sure she was meant for me. I wasn't allowed to date until I was sixteen, so when I heard that Mom had invited her and her family, I was more than willing to help in any way I could to make the whole day a success.

It was approaching 2 o'clock, when they were supposed to arrive. My twelve year old sister, Shirley, and I were sitting on the couch in our Sunday best, having been given strict instructions not to do anything to mess up the house or soil our clothes.

Mom was in the kitchen making last minute preparations to a meal she had never cooked before. Every other year it had been ham or turkey. But this year, the first time we had out of town guests, the first time my potential girlfriend was eating at our table, the first time I had ever worn a coat and tie to a meal, Mom had decided to serve manicotti. I had never heard of manicotti, but Mom had found a recipe in *Better Homes & Gardens* and thought it would make the special meal 'extra special.'

Mom summoned me from the kitchen, "Larry, will you come in here and see if the manicotti is done?"

"Sure, Mom, no problem." Somehow I had become the manicotti expert. A few days earlier I couldn't spell it, but now, apparently, I had absorbed enough culinary expertise from the cosmos to be able to determine the nuances of an Italian dish by merely looking at it. Not that I minded. Dad would say that it needed more ketchup, and Shirley would say it needed more Tabasco.

I tried to venture a somewhat intelligent response. "Oh, boy, Mom, I think that is the best one yet."

"Best *what* yet?" she inquired.

"You know, the best one of *these*." I motioned to the mystery dish.

"The best one of *these... what?*" she motioned me to move along with my comments.

I was in a corner with nowhere to turn but to tell the truth, and that was not a viable option when talking to my mother about her cooking. "You know, one of these..."

"...manicotti." Shirley whispered from the next room.

"Yeah," I said sheepishly. "One of those...manicotti things...foods...dishes...."

Now, don't get me wrong, I loved Mom's cooking. It had made me the robust young man that I was. Her food was good and hot and there was plenty of it. But her style could be described by saying...what Picasso was to art, Mom was to cooking. She had a way of taking a recipe, dissecting it, rearranging it, and making it her own. It was always good and nutritious, but it was just...well...different.

"Well, this manicotti *thing* will have to suffice," she said. "I don't have time to make another meal." She took the pan and put it back in the oven on low heat to stay warm. Then she went into the living room where Dad had set up a piece of plywood on two sawhorses to make a dining table. (We didn't have a dining room.) Then she smoothed a nice sky-blue bed sheet on, to act as the table cloth.

Shirley peeked around the corner of the door of the kitchen and said. "Nice going, Noodlehead." Then she smiled.

I tried to feign taking offense, but all I could do was smile back. Shirley had always had my back since she was old enough to talk. "Noodles I can understand," I joked. "All that manicotti *is*, is a giant noodle." Then I added, "How bad can it be? We always have peanut butter."

"Don't even think that," Shirley whispered. "Mom thinks that peanut butter is the root of all Neanderthals, like you and Dad."

"And you," I added defensively.

"Maybe so," she answered. "But unlike you, I don't make it a *main dish*."

"Kids, come in here, and tell me what you think."

Mom needed some positive re-enforcement and we were only too happy to oblige.

"Oh, Mom," Shirley exclaimed.

"Yes. Oh, Mom," I echoed.

The impromptu table was set with eight place settings of real china, polished tableware (which Shirley and I had so lovingly shined) cloth napkins, and cut-glass water goblets which Mom had borrowed from Grandma Miller. In the middle of the table were matching cut-glass candle holders, with tall, pale blue candles.

"Yes, Mom, it is lovely," I said.

She arched her eyebrows, "Lovely?"

"It's a new word I have been working on." I loved words. So every once in a while I would try one on to see if it fit.

"Thanks, Son," Mom replied, as she scurried into the kitchen for last minute preparations. But the minute turned into minutes and I could tell my mother was nervous.

"I hope they come soon," she said. But they didn't. The 2 o'clock arrival time came and went. Ten after two rolled on by, then twenty after, then it was 2:30. Dad was starting to get mad. We had two solid weeks of getting ready for, as Dad called it, 'Dinner with the Pope,' and he was suspect of its necessity in the first place. Why couldn't we have our traditional Thanksgiving Dinner with the Grandparents Miller?

Finally, in frustration, Dad said, "I think I should call them to see if something has delayed them."

"I think that is a good idea," Mom replied, "But I think it is best if I call. I think you are too upset."

"I'm not upset," Dad bellowed. "I'm mad!"

"My point exactly," she said calmly, as she picked up the phone.

Dad, who was dressed in his Sunday best with a necktie no less, huffed and puffed, and stomped outside to see how the animals were doing.

Mom called, but there was no answer. She considered that a good sign. Perhaps they were on their way and had taken a wrong turn.

"Larry, will you go to the freezer and bring in the ice cream?" Mom asked.

It was a strange request. We hadn't even eaten the meal yet, and she wanted me to get out the dessert.

It would melt before the 'Pope' arrived. But in the nervous state Mom was in, I decided not to point out the obvious.

I went out on the kitchen porch and opened the lid of the freezer chest. Every farmer had a freezer. Most of them didn't can food much anymore so they froze their meat and vegetables. I began to rearrange the contents of the very full freezer to get at the ice cream which was conveniently at the bottom.

First there was a shoebox with a rubber band around it. That is where Mom kept all of the important papers. Something about, in case there was a house fire, the contents of the freezer would survive. Next there was the frozen laundry. In Colorado, between sand storms and snow flurries, there were only a few days a week that clothes could be dried on the line. So, to discourage mildew, Mom would wash clothes in the old wringer washer and then freeze them until the right day came along. There was more than one time that I went to school smelling like frozen hamburger or green beans. It wasn't until I went to college that I found out that none of my classmates had mothers who froze their laundry.

I found the ice cream at the very bottom, where I knew it would be. I carefully replaced the contents and closed the lid. Back in the house, Mom told me to put the ice cream in the refrigerator ice box. Now I understood the method in her madness, although I sincerely hoped it had not turned into madness.

I walked in to our *new* dining room and noticed that not all of the condiments were in place. Without thinking, I called out, "Mom, you forgot to put the peanut butter on the table." Instantly I realized my mistake. Shirley leaned around the corner of the door to the kitchen and hissed at me. She looked just like a cat that was poised to pounce on an unsuspecting mouse.

From the kitchen I heard, "Larry, how can you be so dense?" Actually it was easy. I *was* a Neanderthal after all. "You know we don't serve peanut butter at a nice, sit-down meal." I was already having pangs of peanut butter withdrawal. All of my earliest culinary memories included peanut butter. We used it on toast, hamburgers, and baked potatoes – all kinds of potatoes. Mom used it on meatloaf as her magic ingredient. But Shirley took the cake, literally, when she made a lemon peanut butter cake with a cream cheese peanut butter frosting with peanuts sprinkled on top. Now that was a dessert that stayed with you! Mmm-mmm. As I began drooling, Shirley left the room rolling her eyes, as if to say, '*I want a new sibling.*'

It was approaching three o'clock, and still no pastor or beautiful daughter. I could feel the tension level was rising in the house, so I went outside to find to find out how Dad was doing with the cows. He and the cows were just fine. I found him leaning against a wood fence near the barn. I joined him as we watched the sun in its journey toward the Rocky Mountains.

"It's going to break your mother's heart if they don't come," he said, while he chewed on a piece of wheat straw. "I have never seen her put so much effort into having everything perfect for one meal. Why, she even followed the recipe this time." I could attest to that, being a manicotti inspector and all.

He continued. "To think, we could have been with family." That would have been nice. Uncle Bill and Aunt Mary were to have come from Greeley today to have Thanksgiving with the grandparents and Uncle Roy and his family. Mary was my father's younger sister. She had married a banker from Greeley, and that was Uncle Bill. They often drove out to family events in their 1927 Model 'A,' weather permitting. Uncle Bill was a teller of tall tales and a practical joker. Yes, that would have been nice, but it looked as if we were going to spend *this* Thanksgiving alone.

"Come on, Son, I'm going to put a stop to this," Dad said with resolve.

I followed him into the house, where he picked up the phone and dialed. Mom had already retreated into the bedroom in tears. He said a few words and hung up. He turned to Shirley and me and said he had finally got through to the pastor who had mistaken the appointment for next week. Dad said that he had informed him that there would be *no* next week. Dad went back to the phone while Shirley and I quietly retreated to the couch and turned on the television with the volume low.

Mom came out of her room a few minutes later, face flushed but composed.

"Well, what do you say we eat this meal before it gets even colder?" she said through a forced smile. Dad came out of the kitchen with two cookies bulging out of his cheeks.

"Fnrg…What?" he said, cookie crumbs flying. "Ife waths hungery!"

Shirley smiled, looked at him, and said,

"Neanderthal."

Mom began putting the extra place settings away. Dad swallowed and said, "Why don't you hold up on that."

"Why?" she said.

"We are *hungry*. The kids and I will clean up after we eat." That was a first. Mom couldn't pass up an offer like that. So we sat down to eat.

Just then there was a knock at the door. I opened it... and there was Uncle Bill. "I hear you are serving manicotti today and you didn't invite *me*." He put on a pouty face, and then gently pushed his way into the living room. He had two large paper bags, one under each arm. It looked and smelled like he was carrying delicious leftovers from his previous meal. Behind him was Aunt Mary carrying a baby and more food. Shirley rushed to help with the baby. I moved to help with the food.

As they stood to greet the unexpected guests, Mom urgently whispered to Dad, "Did you..."

"Yes, I did," he interrupted. Then he said in a hushed tone, "By the way, I really appreciate you." For a moment I thought that more tears were coming.

As soon as everyone was somewhat settled, Uncle Bill said, "Did you know that my mother was Italian and she fixed manicotti almost every meal?" We all knew that wasn't true. He wasn't Italian, and if he had manicotti every day his mother would have been cooking all day – every day.

"What are you doing here?" Shirley asked. She was obviously unaware of the fabrication that was taking place.

"Why, we're hungry," he said gesturing to all in attendance.

"Didn't you just eat at Grandma's?" she persisted.

"Why, sure," he said, "But you know your Grandma. She never really fixes enough for us hungry men."

Shirley started to defend Grandma, then realized what was going on.

"Neanderthal," I whispered. I received a little sharp elbow in my ribs for that.

When everyone was seated Mom slipped into the kitchen and brought out the manicotti, which was by now quite dry and burnt around the edges. And she brought out another jar of something or other. Dad said the blessing and at the 'amen,' Uncle Bill said, slyly, "Larry, would you please pass the peanut butter?"

LIFE IN BLACK AND WHITE

by Larry Wayne Miller

"A little to the left," Dad instructed. "No…a little to the right. Now turn and raise your left arm and face Denver. There, that's just right – now put you right foot in. No, that's not quite it. Put your right foot out. No, that's not it either."

Then my little six year old sister Shirley jumped in and sang, "…You put your right foot in and you shake it all about. Do the Hokey Pokey…."

"Dad!" I howled, in indignation.

This had to be the most humiliating moment of

my heretofore humiliating childhood to this point.

Two weeks earlier we had acquired our first television. With great fanfare, Dad had presented it to the family. He got it from the local junk dealer, Estel Reed. It was one of the original Philco television sets which had the round screen encased in a rectangular plastic covering. It wasn't much to look at, but it was a TV. Best of all, it was OUR TV! We were one of the last families in the valley to get one. We didn't have indoor plumbing, but now, we did have a television!

This was in the summer of 1957 and I was eight years old. We lived in the town of Weldona in northeastern Colorado. Now that we had TV, the world was at our finger tips. We were a part of the cultured world of the Fifties. We could watch "I Love Lucy," "The Honeymooners," and "Big Time Wrestling." There was only one problem - the reception was poor. Very poor.

Denver was only 90 miles away, and the plains were so flat that you could almost see it. But try as we might, the screen was grainy and punctuated with squiggly lines.

Dad tried everything. He adjusted the rabbit ears, hung tin-foil from them, and ran a wire from the clothes line. (Mom was afraid that the *Gamma Rays* that television towers give off might fry the clothes.) Ultimately nothing worked. We had to settle for a distorted, snowy picture that leaned to the left.

I watched in amazement as my normally thoughtful, intelligent family sat leaning at a 45 degree angle to the left, while eating TV dinners, and asking pointed questions, such as, if Desi and Lucy were really husband and wife, why did they have different last names?

For some unknown reason the signal changed throughout the evening as it came the ninety miles from Denver to our house. Each half hour one member of the family would take their turn refocusing the rabbit ears. So one night, as I took my turn, Dad exclaimed, "Larry! Stop! That's the best it has ever been!"

I took my hands off the rabbit ears and proceeded to sit down.

"You must have bumped something," Dad said. I turned to look, and he was right. I took hold of the rabbit ears again and adjusted them until he said, "Stop! You've got it." As I turned to go to my seat, he sang out, "You did it again."

"But, I didn't do anything," I said in exasperation.

"Well, try one more time," he said. The instant I touched the rabbit ears, the TV reception was perfect. When I took my hand off, the reception was bad. Hands on...perfect. Hands off...fuzzy. Hands on...clear. Hands off...distorted. Hands on...well, you get the picture. .

I turned just in time to see my little sister say, to no one in particular, "He's an antenna. My big brother is a human antenna."

Dad and Mom, sitting on either side of the couch, looked at me bug-eyed like I was some kind of space alien. My six year old nemesis sat between them grinning from ear to ear, mocking me with scarecrow impersonations.

"What?" I said, spreading my arms in a questioning gesture and accidentally brushing the rabbit ears.

"Stop!" they shouted in chorus. "Don't move!"

After that, I watched incredulously while the three of them laughed at the show, finished their TV dinners, and generally had a good time. Not for a minute did they notice that their family member was standing with a rabbit ear in one hand and an arm outstretched towards Denver with the other, and occasionally, upon demand, doing the Hokey Pokey.

This went on for quite some time until I dared to say "Ahem! Excuse me. Did you forget something?"

At which point, Dad said, "Oh, I'm sorry, Son. I was just so excited to see a clear picture, I forgot you were there. Here, come on over and sit down."

Well, good. I didn't have to stand there looking stupid anymore.

Dad continued, "You can just come over here until the commercial is over, then you can go on back to your place."

I looked at him in disbelief. If this had been thirty years later I would've raised a verbal objection. But this was the Fifties, and we were in the middle of nowhere, living on a dirt farm. I was the Son, and he was the Father. Arguing wasn't an option.

I continued through the evening, exploring my new role as a human receiver. We tried experiments like hanging tin-foil and clothes hangers from my arms. I found that when I faced northwest and touched the pot bellied stove with a clothes hanger, we could pick up a little station in Cheyenne, Wyoming.

But when it came right down to it, it wasn't the tin-foil, and it wasn't the clothes hangers. It was me. No one else in the family could make the TV work. This went on for several evenings, with me standing spread-eagled while the family explored the new and exciting world of television.

Although it was backbreaking work, and I was developing a stiff neck, I was still learning a lot about the emerging world of the Fifties, because I could at least hear the TV.

About this time, Dad discovered the Wonderful World of Channel Flipping. Soon, he got tired of getting in and out of the big easy chair to change the channels. So, always the inventor, he took an old broom handle and cut a grove in it that would slide over the channel changer. Thus he could change the channels while seated. He would sit in his big chair and hold his channel changer, round end on the floor, grooved end up, looking for all the world like a king (in overalls) on his throne.

Actually that solution was fun for a while. I got to interact with the family and speculate what the next show would be about. During all of this, my little sister was torn between two emotions. On one hand she was amused at the contorted poses I had to assume between getting the Denver and Cheyenne stations. But on the other hand, her adored big brother was being treated like an electronic appendage by her beloved father. She even tried to take my spot on occasion. But no combination of aluminum foil and wire clothes hangers could make up for the magnetic personality of her receptive sibling.

All of this worked fine, for about a week, until there was an in-house rebellion. After a commercial I put my hands on my hips and just stood there. As the show resumed, Dad looked at the snowy picture, then looked at me and said, "What!?" (Sometimes Dad could be, well, frankly, *dense*.)

I tried to put a humorous twist to my response. "Dad," I said gently. "I can't do this forever." Then I smiled and continued, "Eventually I will have to go to college, get married, have children...."

He looked baffled...confused...disconcerted. Then he brightened. "But that won't be for another twelve years yet." *So ... dense.*

Mom came to my defense, "You have to admit Marion, ummmm, that at some point, ummm, we have to come up with a better solution."

Dad grinned, "You mean, before college."

Then he did something unexpected. He stood up, came over to the TV, and motioned for me to take his place on the couch. As I did so, he took my place and began an exaggerated series of contorted poses, each more comedic that the last.

"Did I really look that bad?" I exclaimed to no one in particular.

"Actually, *much* worse," my sister chirped.

We were all amused and entertained during the next thirty minutes as Dad tried to get a better picture. We all had to admit that his pictures were almost as good as mine. "This is really difficult," he said during one commercial.

"No kidding," I mumbled.

Then Dad put up his right index finger and

smiled. "I have a New Idea!"

Those were some of the most terrifying words in the Miller household. It usually meant that something that was privately amusing was about to become publicly humiliating.

True to form, Dad's New Idea, which he had adamantly refused to share with us that evening, began to take shape after chores the next morning. First he dug out an old bed springs from our 'Machinery Row.' (An euphemism based on the fact that farmers never threw anything away, they just put them in long rows behind the barn in case they ever needed them for parts. Farmer's wives hated them. Farmers revered them, knowing that they reflected a sense of growing with the times, yet a well-grounded reality that all machines break down. You never knew when you would need that part!)

But, I digress. So, next, Dad had me rub off the rust with a wire brush, while he rummaged around for all of the old aerosol paint cans he could find. Alas, the only ones that still worked were bright silver paint that had been purchased the previous year to repair some metal roofing. We had painted the bed springs with the paint and were letting it dry in the sun when I got my first inkling that something was amiss.

I was admiring the stark beauty of our work, thinking it could be put in the Denver Museum of Modern Art, when Dad said, "Larry, you get the log chain and I'll start up the International 'M' with the loader. We're going to put the bed springs in that cottonwood tree next to the house."

"Wh-wh-what?" I stammered. "What for?"

"We're going to put a wire on it and run it into the house and connect it to the television. It's going to be our new antenna!"

We're What!? NO! Oh no, no, no! That was in front of the house...near the road...where all of the neighbors drove by. It was where the school bus stopped, twice, every day. The school bus that was filled with all of my friends! They already thought that I was weird, that my family was weird. (Except for my sister Shirley. They thought she was cool. And they felt sorry for her. I could hear them in my mind, 'Poor cool Shirley. She's stuck with that family with the silver bed springs in the tree.')

I had hoped that when Shirley saw what Dad was about to do, she would side with me and implore Dad to rethink the idea. But no-no-no-no-no! Her response was, "Cool! Very Cool! I Love It! I'll bet we're the first in the valley to have one!"

No kidding!

I was sinking into a morose state of self- pity when Dad said, "Son, get a move on, we haven't got all day."

Didn't we? How do you tell your highly intelligent, very inventive father, "Dad. Nobody of any class puts silver bed springs in their cottonwood trees."

But as I have said, to dissent was to regret. I spent the next hour helping Dad put the bed springs in the tree, adjusting it to point to Denver and sending a wire into the house.

Almost immediately neighbors started slowing their cars as they approached our house. They rolled down their windows, arms pointing to the *tree*, gawking, laughing...oh, the humiliation! It wasn't long until valley folk who never drove by our house were moseying on by. Dad seemed oblivious to the constant stream of mocking faces that was passing in front of our house. He just waved at each vehicle as it passed by, smiling, nodding, pointing to the shiny contraption in the tree as if it were a brand new tractor.

"Larry, I think people like our new invention," he said, as we took down the ladder and put away the tools. I was too mortified to respond. "There might be some money to be made if this works," he enthused.

A wave of sarcasm washed over my humiliated spirit. "Or maybe...people would pay to just sleep in our tree!" I shouldn't have said it. It wasn't as if this hadn't happened for as long as I could remember. Dad was the most enthusiastic and engaged when he was creating. His inventiveness knew no bounds.

The only problem was come Monday, I would be the butt of everyone's jokes. The whole school would know. Arrrgh!

I was interrupted from my pity party by Grandpa Miller driving into the farm yard in his pickup truck. He parked at the base of the bed spring-cottonwood tree, got out, looked up and exclaimed, "What in the heck is that?" (Well, actually, he didn't say '*heck*.')

That just about summed it up!

Dad's enthusiasm noticeably waned. His relationship with his father had always been a bit strained. Being the oldest Miller Man, Dad was expected to be an example of a hard work ethic, which he was; and thrifty, within the bounds of running a successful farm. Dad had the thrifty part down. And, a Miller Man had to be a serious, no-nonsense practitioner of stern discipline and practical ethics. In other words, Dad was supposed to be just like his father...but better.

Dad never did get that part right. He had a creative, mischievous side that stretched from dawn to sunset. He was always thinking of how to do things better, and there, in a cottonwood tree was his latest example. Under it was *his* father, hands on hips, a scowl on his face. Dad sheepishly approached the tree, bracing himself for a scolding.

At first I hoped that Grandpa would say something that would convince Dad to remove this hideous contraption from the neighbors' prying eyes, but as I followed Dad to the tree of shame, I began to feel defensive for him. Darn it, what was wrong with putting silver bed springs in trees?

"I just got a call from Jim, the corn seed salesman, and he said I just had to see this," Grandpa grumbled. "So now I'm seeing it and I'm open for a, ahem, a *reasonable* explanation."

Grandpa had always treated me much better than he did Dad. I don't know, maybe it was the oldest grandchild thing. So while Dad cranked up his courage, I jumped in - uninvited, impertinent, and dripping with schmaltz.

"It's an antenna, Grandpa." He looked again to the bed springs in the tree and then at me. He didn't like impertinence, he didn't like children speaking out of turn, and he certainly didn't like schmaltz!

"It's a bed springs," he scowled.

"No, it's definitely an antenna," I grinned.

Grandpa gave Dad a look that said, *'Are you going to control this child or not?'*

Dad turned to me and gave me a more panicked look that said, *'What are you doing?'*

I forged on, "What you see before you is Dad's latest invention, the Coil Wire Super Antenna."

Grandpa was done being jerked around by a snot-nosed kid. "It's a bed springs!"

"It would be if someone was sleeping on it," I joked. "But it's in a tree and its pointing toward Denver."

Dad gave me another *look*. It said, *'If he doesn't end your life...I will!'*

Shirley, unbeknownst to us, had stood nearby and heard the entire farce. With a big grin on her face she said, "Why don't you come in and see how it works Grandpa?" Now *I* was the one who gave Shirley the, *'Are you out of you mind?'* look.

A sly grin enveloped Grandpa's face. "Why, sure...don't mind if I do."

Dad stood rigidly as all the blood drained from his face. He tried to speak but nothing would come out. Grandpa had already started for the house so I gently took Dad's elbow and aimed him to follow.

Grandpa had only been in our house a handful of times, but he had no problem finding the living room and our decrepit round screen TV. Mom had already fled the scene and barricaded herself in the back bedroom. She wanted no part of this. Shirley stood beside the television as if she were a game show hostess and Grandpa stood impatiently in front of it.

Dad, who had partially regained himself, turned on the television and said nervously, "It takes a while to warm up the tubes."

"I know *that*," Grandpa growled. "I have a *new* one in my house." Then he added, with glee, "And I *didn't* buy it in a junk yard." I had to go and restrain my sister so she couldn't kick him in the shins.

Dad hooked the copper wire to the antenna screw and - wonder of wonders - it worked…a little. The picture was fuzzy and leaned to the left, but it worked.

"Well, I'll be darned," Grandpa said. "That's better than our new TV."

And so it was, but it still leaned to the left and it was a little grainy.

"But it leans to the left, and it's a little grainy," he continued.

My thoughts exactly.

Then Shirley, who was always two steps ahead of everything and everyone, said, "Larry, why don't you go over and tighten the wire. It looks like it has come a little loose."

I looked at the wire. It looked fine to me. I said, "It looks fine to me."

Shirley hissed through clenched teeth, "I think *zee* wire is a little *loose*." She jerked her head aggressively towards the television. I finally got it!

I turned to Grandpa, accidentally caught in the moment, and said through clenched teeth, "I zink the zee wire is loose. I zink I will just go over and fix it."

Grandpa scanned the room and its participants

and his gaze rested on Dad. "I *zink* there are a lot of loose wires loose in zis room."

We all chuckled nervously as I hurried to the antenna wire. As soon as I touched it the picture was better than it had ever been!

Grandpa nodded in approval. "I'm going to tell the boys down at the Co-op. They'll never believe this." With that, he left and we all breathed a communal sigh of relief.

"You know," Dad said, tilting his head to the left, "This is a really good picture. Only," he said, tilting his head to the other side, "It would be even better if you would…Put your right foot in…put your right foot out…."

"DAD!" Shirley and I shrieked in unison.

Over the next few weeks, bed springs started migrating into cottonwood trees all over the valley. Most people swore that their reception was better instantly. But then something weird happened.

Unmarked government vehicles began stopping at the houses of families with bed springs in their trees. Pairs of nondescript men wearing sunglasses and matching cheap suits began asking pointed questions. "Why are you people putting up *advanced listening antennas* in your trees?"

"What?" these people said. "These are just bed springs. They make our TVs work better."

Then the 'G' men, as they became known around the valley, pulled out pictures of Soviet listening arrays that were pointed at all of the US military bases around the world. They looked suspiciously like bed springs in cottonwood trees. "So, why are these listening arrays pointed at Colorado Springs and the Air Force Base there?"

The bed springs all over the valley began coming down as fast as they had gone up. But the 'Feds' asked one more question. "Who put you up to this? Who told you to put listening arrays in your trees?"

You guessed it. They reported unanimously. "It was him! That Marion Miller, down the road a piece."

So it came to pass that one morning, a nondescript sedan drove into our yard. Two men with sunglasses and cheap suits came to the door of our farm house and asked for Marion Miller. I pulled into our yard a few moments later on our Minneapolis 'Z' tractor. (*Yes*, I drove a tractor *that young;* all the farm boys did.) In moments, I caught sight of the sedan. I looked around. Dad wasn't there. Mom was nowhere to be found. I knew what was going on, so I rushed into the living room to see if I could help.

But Shirley already had everything under control. She had one of the 'G' men standing next to the TV holding the rabbit ears. We still had them attached, in addition to the bed springs.

"Wow," he was saying, "This really works…and all because of a silly bed springs and some rabbit ears!"

But Shirley couldn't resist. She said, grinning from ear to ear, "Now…put your right foot in…put your right foot out…."

FISHIN'

by Larry Wayne Miller

"Whatchadoin'?"

"Practicing."

That was not the answer I was expecting.

Shirley, my little sister, was sitting at the edge of the Weldon Valley irrigation ditch in front of our farm house in Weldona, Colorado. She held a long stick with a string tied on the end. A red and white bobber was attached to the string. The whole contraption barely made a dent in the massively muddy mess below. If she was doing what I *thought* she was doing, she was trying to catch mud carp. Those robust little icky fish had earned their reputation of being nasty looking, nasty acting, and nasty tasting fish. So, why?

"I mean, what are you doing with the stick and bobber and stuff?" I rephrased.

"I'm fishing, as you can see." She sounded put out by my lack of perception of the clearly obvious.

I detected the irritation and said, kindly and gently, "But, *why* are you doing it?"

"I'm practicing."

I thought she said she was fishing!

"For what?"

"To catch a fish, silly."

Now *I* was becoming irritated.

"But why here?"

"Because this is water and there are fish in there," my little sister said.

Technically she was correct. It *was* water and there *were* fish in there. But it wasn't a river, it wasn't a lake, and the fish, in reality, weren't edible.

This was the summer of 1961. I was twelve years old, and although I lacked Shirley's cognitive agility, I was far superior in worldly acumen. Of course, at that age, I had no idea what any of that meant. Nevertheless, I jumped in with both feet.

"Sis, that *water* you are *practicing* in is an *irrigation ditch*. The only fish that live in it are vile, nasty tasting mud carp. They are swimming in so much silt that I doubt that they can even see your worm."

"Worm?"

"You didn't use a worm?"

"You need a worm?"

I eyed her incredulously. This whole conversation had taken place while Shirley's back was turned to me as she kept a steady eye on the bobber.

"Are you eyeing me incredulously?"

"I have no idea what that means."

"It means you are dubious of my actions," she explained.

"I have no idea what that means either," I lamented.

She turned quickly and looked me straight in the eye. "Are you lamenting the fact that you don't know any big words?" Then she gave me that mischievous little 'I love to make fun of you in private, big brother, but you know I always have your back in public,' look.

It was true. At ten years old, Shirley was precocious, funny, and articulate. She said, "You're wondering why I am sitting on the Weldon Valley irrigation ditch bank trying to catch fish that are yucky and live basically in mud, and why I am sitting on ground that is likely to be infested with rattlesnakes, mice, and mosquitoes."

I pondered for a millisecond. "Yep, that's it in a nutshell."

She returned to concentrating on the bobber. "The new pastor's wife has been telling us in Sunday School how relaxing and meditative fishing is. Apparently she used to do a lot of it in her earlier years."

The new pastor and his wife had been working overtime, trying to fit in with their new parish. Most people appreciated the effort, but what the new pastor and his wife *didn't* realize was that they didn't need to try nearly so hard. The little town of Weldona accepted everybody, as long as they made an honest effort. There were only two churches in town. You were either a Catholic or everything else. We were an 'everything else.'

Continuing to display my worldly acumen, and the fact that I did, indeed, attend school, I said, "I thought meditation was for those eastern religions."

Although still viewing the back of Shirley's head, I thought I detected a smirk.

"Not bad, big brother. You are partially correct." *Ah! Justified by a superior being.* "But meditation is just the practice of letting go of all distractions and concentrating on something that brings you peace."

I began thinking of things on the farm that brought me peace. Driving a tractor. Cultivating knee-high corn down an endless, lonely row. Hearing a stream of steaming milk, fresh from the udder, hit the creamy froth in a galvanized bucket held gently but firmly between my knees. That was the kind of thing I found peaceful.

"Whoa!"

"Whoa?"

"Yes, whoa!" Shirley uttered.

"Whoa what?"

"I think I've hooked something!"

End of meditation time, kiddies!

"I thought you didn't use a worm," I exclaimed.

"Maybe I was playing with you." She screeched while the flimsy willow pole bent over double.

"Well, maybe you can play with your little mud carp, then," I hissed, starting to walk away.

"Don't even think about it, Larry! Get down here and help me!"

Ah, to be needed.

Taking a quick glance to make sure I wasn't stepping on any meditating snakes, I hurried to her side to help her pull in the monster of the deep. The little willow branch looked as if it was about to break. The only thing that kept it intact was its reputation of being, well, willowy.

"Point the stick toward the fish," I suggested. To Shirley's credit she didn't ask me 'why?' She just did as I asked.

"Now, start winding the string around the pole the way you would if you were winding in a kite," I encouraged.

"You do realize that a fish weighs considerably more than balsa wood and paper," she said through gritted teeth.

I did realize that, though I ignored the comment and gingerly reached for what was, for all practical purposes, simple cotton string. "What kind of hook did you use?" I inquired.

"Hook?" she asked.

There she was, in the middle of reeling in a monster of from the deep, and she was messin' with me again!

As I eased my hands onto the taut cotton string, I

could feel the cool ooze of the ditch water passing between my fingers. It was an unpleasant reminder of what wrestling an angry, muddy cat fish was going to be like.

I didn't try to take over and bring in the fish myself. I wanted Shirley to do that. But I did take some of the tension off of the string so she could continue winding it in.

Suddenly the big slimy fish appeared! It was slimy and ugly, indeed, but most of all it was big. Really big!

"Wow!" Shirley muttered.

"Wow!" I echoed.

The big fish opened its cavernous mouth as if to concur. Then it was gone. All that remained was a large safety pin.

Then it was me who stood with mouth open. "You really *didn't* have a hook," I stated.

"No," she smiled demurely.

"You didn't have a worm, either," I continued.

"No," she grinned.

"You didn't have a clue, did you?"

"No." By now her ecstasy knew no bounds. "But Larry!" she exuded, "I caught a fish! I really, really caught a fish! And it was a big one! Can you believe it?"

Actually, I could believe it. If there was anyone in the world who deserved to catch a monster fish, with no hook, no worm, and no clue, it was my sister.

"Isn't fishing fun!" she bubbled.

I looked at the slime on my hands, which had also splattered all over my shirt and pants. "Yeah, fun," I agreed, wiping my muddy hands on my pre-soiled shirt, "This is *Great Fun.*"

If she caught the sarcasm, she didn't show it. She just took her willow pole, her string, her red and white bobber, and her bent safety pin and headed for the house.

I rushed to catch up, checking for stinging things and biting things.

Over her shoulder she intoned, "Next I think I'll take up fly fishing."

"Fly fishing?"

"Yes, fly fishing. I checked out a book at the school library. I know all about it."

Knowing Shirley, I'm sure she did.

"Good luck with that," I said.

"With what?" she asked.

"With catching a fly," I grinned.

She furrowed her brow and looked at me as one looks at a obnoxious puppy.

"It's not that kind of fly," she intoned. "You make it out of a hook and various scraps around the house."

I hated all flies. Especially ones around the house.

When we got to the porch, Mom met us at the door. "What on earth have you two been doing?" she exclaimed. She looked at my muddy, yucky condition and then she *smelled* my muddy, yucky condition.

She was just about to say something when Shirley interjected, "We caught a fish, a big one! And it was in the irrigation ditch all the time."

Instead of saying, "Oh, Shirley isn't that

wonderful," or "How clever of you," she said, "Larry, how could you!"

I just stood there dripping muddy ditch water, shamed into silence.

"Don't you know that there are snakes and rats and ticks!"

Oh My!

"You're supposed to be watching out for your little sister."

"And," Shirley went on, as if Mom had not spoken at all, "It was *this* big!" She stretched her arms as wide as she could and held them there, waiting for the anticipated response of approval.

"Well, isn't that amazing," Mom said, putting her arm around Shirley's shoulders and gently leading her inside the house. "Come on in. I'll make some hot chocolate and we'll talk about it."

I began to follow, but Mom turned to me and said, "Not you, Mud Boy. You need to go to the barn and wash off some of that fish smell. Rinse your clothes and put on the emergency milking clothes we have out there." I headed out to do so.

After chores and a meal of, what else but my mom's favorite meal, *fish sticks*, I went out to the windmill. I leaned on its rusted frame and watched a brilliant Colorado sunset. There was always a breeze on the plains and it drove our windmill which pumped fresh cold water into a trough for the cows to drink. I was lost in thought when a safety pin with downy little chicken feathers attached to it plunked onto the top of the water in the trough beside me. Attached to the pin was the same string and pole I had seen just a few hours earlier. Attached to the pole was my sister. Attached to her face was smug little smile.

"Whatchadoin'?" she asked. Was she mocking me?

I grinned, deciding it was all in good fun. There's nothing like the feeling of having a little sister who thinks you are the 'best brother in the whole wide world!'

"I'm meditating," I replied.

That brought a twinkle to her eye as she cast the pole, string, and makeshift fly back and forth, trying to hit the same spot in the water tank each time.

"The idea is to make the fish think there is an insect hovering just above the water, waiting to be eaten," she said, concentrating on her casting.

The cows who had wandered over to get a drink wanted nothing to do with the distraction of a fly in their water, fake or not. They backed off, water dripping from their noses.

She stopped what she was doing and looked straight at me. "Thanks for helping me with my river monster earlier."

"That's the job of big brothers," I countered.

"Is it the job of big brothers to fend off snakes, rats, swarming insects, and river monsters?"

"Yep."

"Is it the job of big brothers to get slimy and stinky in the process?"

"You betcha."

"And is it the job of big brothers to go to the barn and wash off their clothes, scrub themselves down, and change into work clothes, while their little sister is adored, fed cookies and hot chocolate, and asked to tell the fishing story, over and over?"

I put on a fake frown and said, "You put it that way...."

She put down her pole, came over, and gave me a tight hug around the waist. "When I grow up I want to be a big brother," she said.

"Well," I teased, "Don't expect me to be the little sister!"

*   *   *

My wonderful little sister took up fly fishing many years later. Shirley Ann Miller is an avid fly fisher and always releases what she catches. She is a member of several fishing clubs and supports many fishing organizations. And yes, she still is cognitively superior, despite my increased worldly acumen.

GLEANING

by Larry Wayne Miller

It was late in November of 1960. It had been a cold wet fall and it would be another month until all of the crops that could still be harvested would be put away for the season. Added to that was the fact that the winter which was to become known as 'The Big Hard Cold,' had set in a month early. A good part of our feed corn crop lay in the field, frozen in time like a Salvador Dali landscape against a steel gray northeastern Colorado sky. It would be late March before there was even a small reprieve.

I was eleven years old that fall and as soon as the school day was over at the Weldon Valley School, I got on the school bus, trudged to my regular seat, and threw my book pack and lunch pail on it. I stepped over the tangle and slumped against the cool yellow metal. It was the coolness that I desired. The school had been hot. School was always hot. I spent so much of my time outside on the farm that the coolness of the bus and the chill of the metal around the window helped sooth my worried mind.

It was the end of the school day, but just the continuation of the farm day which had started long before sunup and would end well after sundown. I was old enough to realize that things were not going well on the farm. That was a large part of what had me worried. A poor harvest, corn still frozen in the field, and lower prices for commodities meant, as Uncle Roy would say, 'slim pickin's' this winter. Dad had taken on as many extra jobs as he could find, but this time of year, every one was vying for those same jobs. He had kept a brave face but I knew that it was eating him up.

"Is this seat taken?" I turned from my brooding to see my little nine year old sister, Shirley, standing there with her, 'I love you, big brother,' smile. I smiled back and moved my stuff to make room for her and *her* stuff.

"Something bothering you?" she asked.

"Oh, just the usual," I answered.

"You have a lot of 'the usual' lately," she teased.

Without thinking, I turned, put my hot face against the cool window of the bus and returned to personal reflection.

"Don't worry," she reassured, "Something will *turnip*."

That was Shirley. The whole family had always loved a 'turn of a word.' We spent endless hours, the four of us, crammed into the cab of a 1949 Chevy pickup truck making poems, impromptu stories, and new verses for old songs. But Shirley was the Champion. Even from an early age she could stand toe-to-toe with Dad, and he was a master. She could quip, quote, pun, and squelch him into submission. In the end, he would grin and shake his head and say, "How old *is* that kid?" He had been beaten by the best.

I turned to Shirley and smiled. "Turnips?"

She knew, as I did, that times were tough. Putting food on the table this winter was going to be a challenge. All the crops we grew were for feeding animals, not people. The one exception was sugar beets, but they had to be processed into sugar first. Sugar beets were considered a cash crop. We were taking a chance in growing it, with all of the bugs and blights that could do it harm. But we knew that if we were able to get it to harvest, it should bring in some good money.

But it hadn't happened that way. Turns out, everyone was growing sugar beets. There was a glut on the market, which meant that the prices barely met expenses.

Not that we would go hungry. Grandma Miller and Uncle Roy would never let that happen. Grandma Miller raised a *HUGE* garden and canned vegetables in dozens and dozens of quart jars.

But Dad was a 'stubborn German,' as Mom would say, and he looked at our want as *his* weakness.

"Yes, turnips," Shirley continued. "They are actually just as nutritious as potatoes, without the side effects."

"Side effects?"

"Don't worry about the details, big brother," she said with a smile. "You will understand it better when you are older."

Shirley's impish grin reminded me of who was really the 'smart one' in the family.

On the way back to the farm, the bus was full of giggling, chattering children. It was a cacophony of sound punctuated by the bus driver shouting instructions, reprimands, and threats. The exception was Shirley. She, as usual, had already started her homework. While she was thus engaged, I studied the frozen landscape, trying to think how I could help the family bring in more of…anything!

I was befuddled. (That was a spelling word the teacher was making us use in sentences.) How could an eleven year old boy that was engaged sixteen hours a day have time to bring in anything that he wasn't already bringing?

I was thinking of possibilities when I heard more commotion on the bus, that is, even more than usual. Everyone was coming to my side of the aisle and looking out the window. One of the older boys sneered, "Who are those idiots working on their hands and knees in this weather?"

I looked out of the window and there were

people doing something in a field that had been recently harvested of potatoes.

As if reading my mind Shirley leaned over to me and whispered, "They're gleaning."

I had heard the word in a sentence but I had never tried using it myself. I had no reference. I had never gleaned. I hadn't had the need to.

"That means they are taking perfectly good food from the field that the harvesting machines missed."

"I think I know that," I hissed.

I turned to her expecting to say something snide, but when I looked into Shirley's eyes I could see she was sincerely trying to help her less cognitive big brother.

Although we were taught never to refer to people by the word that the sneering boy had used, there were indeed people of all ages working in the fields, and the temperature was very chilly. As we got closer, the bus began to slow down. Although it wasn't a regular stop, buses in those days would often deliver children to where they or their parents were working. It made it simpler for working families.

"Look at those morons," the obnoxious kid continued. "They should get a job so that they could *buy* food instead of *stealing* it."

Slowly Shirley turned red, then purple, then crimson. Through gritted teeth she said to the boy, "That is your *father's* field. During the day those people work for your *father*. He gave them permission to... *Glean,* that field. *If* ...he paid them a better...*wage*...maybe they wouldn't have to work, in...*fu*...*reeeezing* weather, to *Ga*...*lean* the field, so that they could...*feed* their children."

The boy was mortified. He had been called out by a nine year old girl! The whole bus, including his friends and relatives, erupted in applause. I could see the bus driver in the rear- view mirror. He was grinning from ear to ear.

Slowly, all of the children from families in the fields got up and made their way to the front of the bus. They were clearly embarrassed, all except one of the older boys who made pointed, and challenging eye contact with the boy who had called his people names. When he passed Shirley he patted her shoulder. She smiled.

I leaned over to her and whispered, "Was any of that true?"

"I don't know," she shrugged.

"Well," I said admiringly. "That took..." I stopped myself just in time from saying what I had heard in the boys' rest room.

"Balls..." she said drolly. Then after a beat she added, "I would have thought then, it should have been *you*, that said it!"

Ouch!

As the bus drove away, I could see everyone in the fields coming to greet their children and grandchildren. Then they went back to the field and worked side by side.

By the way, there were no surprises in Weldon Valley in the fifties and sixties. That was because of the marvelous introduction of something called the 'Party Line.' The valley was divided up into areas of service for the telephone system. Our line had eight different families on it. It was part of the lifeline of the Valley. All you had to do was listen for your special ring. Ours was two long and one short.

The unfortunate side effect was that almost everyone else on the line would pick up and listen also. We tried not to say anything personal or revealing over the phone. In fact, most families would develop a personal code, so no one else could understand its meaning. For instance, 'Uncle Bernie drove to Poughkeepsie,' might mean, 'Last night, Uncle Ernie came home tipsy.'

A phone on a party line could also be used as an information gathering device. Just by picking it up, a small click would sound all up and down the line, followed by a number of other little clicks. In essence everyone else on the line would be saying, 'What's Up!'

It wasn't at all uncommon for a farmer to pull into someone else's farm yard several miles away from his own farm, honk the horn on his pickup truck, roll down his window, wait for someone to come and open the screen door, and tell them to get the word out to everyone else on the line that someone's fence was down and there were escaping cows all over the place. It may have been rude, but not all that uncommon.

On this day, Ethel, who was first on the line, would do the cursory click and announce that the bus had just passed her house. She was way past the age of having any children on the bus, but she felt it was her 'God given duty' to inform when anyone was coming up the road, be it school bus, ditch rider, or politician. So by the time the bus got to our house, Mom had at least a ten minute warning.

When we got home Dad was waiting in our 1949 Chevy pickup truck, with the engine running.

"Hop in," he said, as I was walking to the house. I did as I was told, although I was concerned about what might be about to transpire.

At first I thought I was in trouble. Maybe he had something to talk to me about. He started the truck and headed out of the yard.

Now, this was *strange*. As he shifted into third gear, he handed me a brown paper bag and said, "Mom packed you a little snack and there's a bottle of soda in the glove compartment."

Okay, now this was freaking me out! Mom and Dad would never let us have a soda for no reason at all. "What's going on, Dad? Where are we going?"

"Well, you remember how you were wondering how you could help bring in something that would help the family with our shortfall?"

"Sure I remember." I had come up with a few ideas like helping with other people's chores. After my chores were done, of course. Or getting a paper route in Fort Morgan. The only problem was that was thirty-five miles away. None of my ideas were practical. I simply didn't have any extra time. "The offer still stands," I said.

"I know it does," he smiled. "So an opportunity arose that I think you will be excited about."

We were approaching the field where the families were sifting for potatoes.

"So…what is it?" I prompted.

Dad began slowing down the truck. "Today," Dad said expansively. "Together..."

Oh no! Oh God no!

"Side by side...."

Just kill me now!

"We are going GLEANING!"

I buried my face in my hands.

Dad coasted the truck to a stop at the entry to the field. "What's wrong, Son?"

After a moment, I realized how foolish I must look. Dad and I had always had an open and understanding relationship, sometimes, much to his chagrin.

"Dad...it's...just..."

"Spit it out Son. We only have a couple hours of daylight left."

Then it all spilled out. "It's just that the bus came by here a few minutes ago and there were kids on the bus that were kind of...making fun of the people in the field and then the bus stopped and let their children off, and then the boys on the bus started making fun and...." I was at the age when my whole life *was* a run-on sentence.

"I hope," Dad said firmly, "that you weren't involved in making fun at the expense of others?"

"Oh, not me!" I exclaimed.

"And I hope you defended those kids and their hard-working parents." An uncomfortable moment passed.

"Well...actually...it was Shirley."

Dad smiled and then he chuckled. "That sounds like your sister."

He turned off the engine. There was no sound save the familiar sounds of the engine clicking and clacking as it cooled off, and the low moan of the northeastern Colorado wind finding its way around the old Chevy.

After a reflective pause Dad said, "Son, we live life as it is given to us. This year has been our most difficult yet. The owner of these fields has graciously offered to allow anyone who wants to glean all they want." I remembered that in fact, every farmer I knew in the Weldon Valley did the same thing.

"You know why your Uncle Roy and Grandpa Miller never harvest the last two rows of corn in most of our fields?"

I thought about how the animals, birds and even geese flying south for the winter would feed there in the cold difficult months to come.

"To feed the animals for the winter," I offered.

"It's not only that," Dad said. "Those rows are sweet corn, some of it even Indian corn."

I looked at him blankly, not comprehending.

"It's people corn. Where do you think some of the corn bread and tortillas come from in the middle of the winter?"

I nodded my head. I did understand.

Then Dad wound it up. "No one in this valley ever goes hungry. Between the churches, the farmers, and the women's organizations, no one misses a meal."

All of a sudden I felt part of something much bigger than myself. I changed into the work clothes, coats, hats, and gloves that Dad had brought along. Pushing open the truck door, and letting in a blast of cold air, I said, "Let's do this."

Dad and I were greeted by people we had worked with, shoulder to shoulder, all summer long.

He greeted them, "Hola."

They greeted him, "Hello, Mister Marion."

There were a few pleasantries, but, like all those who know the value of work, it was time to get back to the task. Daylight was burnin'.

We chose an area of the field that had not been worked and began the backbreaking work of filling our burlap bags to the top. In those days most produce was transported in burlap bags and so they were plentiful.

The ground was frozen to several inches down, and my gloves got muddy and stuck to the shovel. My boots were a mess! But soon enough, the bag was full. Dad sewed it shut with a thick sisal cord.

When we had filled a few bags, Dad went back to the truck and came back to our work place, pulling an old snow sled. All the people were smiling and pointing. Dad just shrugged.

I noticed that the sled stayed on the top of the partially frozen ground without sinking in very much. Whereas, the child's wagon the others were using had frozen mud on the tires and was very difficult to maneuver over the icy rutted field.

As Dad arrived, I said, "We'll see how well it does with two big bags of potatoes on it."

"Yes *you* will," he quipped.

"I what!?"

He turned the sled so that it was pointing towards our truck and hoisted two big bags of 'spuds' onto it.

"When you get it started, make sure you don't stop until you get to the truck. The runners have mud on them and they will freeze to the field if you dally."

I wrapped the thick rope around my hand and said with a grin, "What if I just dilly?" I was waiting for a recognition of my little joke when he took his big boot and gave the sled and its cargo a mighty shove. All of a sudden I was running to keep up with sled. All the kids in the field and a few of the adults stood immobile for a moment, staring, and then started shouting words of encouragement.

Getting the large, heavy bags into the back of the truck looked like more than I could manage, but I remembered a trick my Uncle Roy had taught me.

My dad kept two eight foot long 2x12 planks in the back of his truck for general purposes. They were beat up and cracked but they were still plenty strong. I pulled the tail gate of the truck down, placed the planks side by side from the box to the ground with just enough room for me to stand between them. Then I simply rolled the bags from the ground into the truck. I could feel a lot of eyes on me as I slowly accomplished the task.

As I pulled the empty sled back to our work place, Dad smiled and nodded his head. That simple gesture was more praise than I could have wanted with a thousand words.

From that moment on I did nothing but transport potatoes on the sled. Dad had two bags filled and sewed up by the time I returned for another trip.

After the third trip he said, "Boy, you've got to slow down. You're working me ragged." A big smile enveloped his face.

All of a sudden this was fun! I forgot the cold. I forgot about the ridicule some of my friends might give me. I forgot that we were poor. If we had lots of money my Dad and I wouldn't be working side by side right now. We would be sitting in a brand new, heated truck sipping hot chocolate, watching other people work.... *Come to think of it, that didn't sound half bad!*

After another round trip Dad said, "Larry, why don't you take five or six of our empty bags to the other folks. It looks like they are running out." He added, "Take the sled with you. It might make their job easier."

I balked until Dad said briskly, "Go on now. I don't have time to explain every decision I make to you!"

I was a little bit hurt. Not for any reason except that I didn't want to compromise the fun I was having with a Dad.

In the course of the afternoon, I learned the names of some of the men. The older man, who seemed to be the patriarch, was named Juvenal. He had many brothers. Two of them, the two who helped most with transporting the sacks of potatoes and loading them into the various vehicles, were named Jose and Jesus, which when pronounced, didn't sound like Jesus at all.

The families were glad to get the extra bags, as the sun was beginning to set over the Rocky Mountains. It seemed that every minute the temperature fell another degree. They, as well as we, still had chores to do before a very late supper and a little homework and finally falling into bed so we could start it all over the next day.

Still, the kids had a great time loading and playing with the sled. In fact, in spite of the cold and challenging conditions, there was a lot of laughter and good natured banter. I didn't understand most words of their language, but my new friend from the school bus, called Juan, interpreted for me. Sometimes he helped me roll the bags of potatoes up the planks and into the truck, too.

As soon as we were finished loading their cars to the brim with 'taters,' Jose and Jesus came and helped us finish loading our truck. Juvenal was standing by, watching.

"Juvenal, I want you to know about another field that you could glean, one you might not be aware of," Dad said. He proceeded to tell them of other fields he knew about, and to exchange news on the women in the respective families.

"Thank you, Mister Marion, " said Juvenal, his accent quite strong. With that, we all went our separate ways to get chores done at home.

Juvenal, Jose, and Jesus became fast friends with us after that. During the rest of the dreary winter one of the three brothers would often drop by. They would bring us casseroles, tamales, enchiladas, and other treats that I couldn't begin to pronounce. On every occasion, Dad would discreetly ask if they could use a few more potatoes. A good part of the time they would say no, but often, they knew of *others* that could use some.

"That's great!" Dad would say. "We have more

than we could ever use."

Actually, I didn't think that was entirely true. We were running short, and at our present rate of consumption, we might run out ourselves. When I shared my concerns with Mom, she said, "We just need to pray about it. There is plenty of food out there. It just needs to get to the right places." Consequently, she shared those concerns on our party line. By the end of the day, food was ricocheting all over the valley.

That Sunday, the preacher changed the words of our hymn, <u>Leaning on the Everlasting Arms.</u> It was great fun to sing, "Gleaning, gleaning, gleaning on the everlasting arms."

The winter of The Big Hard Cold was eventually over. Spring did arrive. But ever after, there was a new season in the valley of Weldona, Colorado. Added to the seasons of Winter, Spring, Summer, and Fall, there was a new season. It was called the season of…Gleaning.

SUNSET

by Larry Wayne Miller

"Larry, tell me what you see, would you, please?"

I was sitting with Aunt Maud on a squeaky metal rocking bench in the tiny town of Weldona watching a brilliant northeastern Colorado sunset as it sank into the Rocky Mountains. Aunt Maud, who was a distant aunt at best, was nevertheless *family*. And family was always an overriding priority in the world of Marion Miller, my father. Now that I was nine years old, Dad occasionally dropped me off at Aunt Maud's to help her with whatever chores she might have. She was wise enough to always have a peanut butter and jelly sandwich with a glass of milk waiting for me before I launched into chores.

On this day, late in the summer of 1958, she had requested that Dad drop me off a little later than usual, just before sunset, so that she could show me something special. The 'something special' turned out to *be* the sunset.

When I arrived, she suggested, since it was so close to supper time, that perhaps I should just stay for a meal. It is well known among nine-year-old boys that senior citizens who live on their own often have weird eating habits. Aunt Maud loved saltine crackers piled high with sardines and Gouda cheese, which left her house filled with a permeating aroma of moldering fish and French caves for days.

I looked up at Dad, with panic stricken eyes. He was bemused but sensed my angst. "Actually," he said, "Jessie and Shirley are waiting up dinner for us, so we can only be a while." Jessie is my mom. Shirley is my sister, seven years old at the time. Having saved my bacon, Dad excused himself, saying he had a few errands to run but would be back in half an hour.

"Oh…that's too bad," Maud said. "It would have been nice to share a meal with someone." She looked wistfully at the setting sun as I took a big bite out of my peanut butter sandwich.

Knowing what to expect eased my mind. I could stand anything, or almost anything, for half an hour.

"There are no chores for today," Maud announced. "I just wanted to share a sunset with someone, and you seemed to be the only one not working at that time."

Actually, I would have been working if it were not for the summons to Aunt Maud's house. I didn't know anyone in the valley who wasn't working or finishing up work at sundown.

"I've fixed some lemonade, instead of milk, to go with your peanut butter sandwich. You will enjoy that, won't you?" I *did* enjoy lemonade… if it was loaded with sugar. Regrettably, Aunt Maud's lemonade was loaded with…lemons.

"So, Larry, tell me what you see." What I could see was what I had seen every day of my young life for as long as I could remember - a big sky Colorado sunset. Some days it was cloudy. Some days there were huge thunderheads, black on the horizon with menacing bolts of lightning reaching out with shocking tendrils. But on this day the sun reigned supreme. There was not a cloud in the sky and the usually strong prairie wind had calmed to a gentle breeze.

Realizing there was a vacuum of silence, I said, "I see a really big red sunset." I spied the big clock on the kitchen wall through the window. Only twenty-six minutes to go.

"Oh, Larry, you can do better than that," she scoffed, followed by a chuckle. "Now, think about some of the names on the crayon box I bought you last Christmas. There were 64 colors. Surely you must remember some of them."

I did remember some of them. "Yellow, blue, green…and…Indian Red," I blurted. I liked Indian Red. Not that I really liked the *color*, I just liked the word Indian in the name. Anything with the word Indian caught my attention at nine years old.

"Really?" She said, squinting into the setting sun. "It looks more like a red-orange to me."

I turned to her. "That sounds like two colors combined."

It is," she said, turning back towards the sunset. "But it *is* part of the crayon box."

During the next twenty minutes, I named all of the colors around us. They were changing by the minute, as the sun slowly drifted into the Rocky Mountains. During that time I had devoured the peanut butter sandwich and downed two glasses of very sour lemonade. I was just standing up to get another glass of lemonade, with just ten minutes to go, when Maud said, "Wait Larry... Just sit with me and enjoy the last moments of this day. There won't be many more days like today."

So, I did. As we gently rocked the squeaky steel bench swing, the sun said its final goodbyes. By that time I had forgotten about the clock on the wall in the kitchen.

"One last thing," she said. "Please, describe the sky, as it is now."

I turned my face up and looked from horizon to horizon, which was easy to do in eastern Colorado.

"I see a very pale yellow, almost like cream, followed by a whisper of blue."

"Oh, Larry, that is quite poetic," she sighed. "Tell me more."

"Then, I don't know... the blue gets darker and darker as it chases the purple into the night." Breathless, I turned toward Maud. She was smiling peacefully with the afterglow of the evening settling on her face. At her request, I left her sitting there, and went quietly home as soon as my dad arrived.

I rolled the window down on my side of our 1949 Chevy farm truck, and put my face on my folded arms on the window sill. The cool evening air danced through my hair as the old truck shifted gears and Dad pulled into the Colorado night. I could feel the crunch of gravel beneath the tires, the whine of the four speed transmission behind the throbbing six cylinder 235 engine. It punctuated the night as two tunnels of light showed us the way home. Dad seemed to understand my mood and let me cradle in it without interruption.

"You are mighty quiet this evening," Mom said, over supper.

Shirley was watching me closely. She was pretty, smart, and extremely 'knowing' for her age. "Hey, brother, what's up?"

"I don't know really. It's just that I watched a sunset with Aunt Maud." But that didn't come close to explaining what I was feeling. So I told them the whole story, how she had asked for more colors and I couldn't give them to her the way I thought she wanted. And how she had sighed and smiled and asked me to just leave her there. "I felt like there was something more I should have done."

Then Dad uttered the first words he had all evening. "Like what, Son?"

"Actually, I had the feeling she was going to die after we left."

Mom gave a gasp.

Dad looked at me for a long while and said, "She's not dying, Son... she's going blind."

I let that sink in for a while. I had never known anyone who was blind, or going blind. "Can she see *anything?*" I asked.

Dad leaned back in the naugahide kitchen chair and looked out through the screen door into the deep Colorado night. "She can see around the edges of her eyes. She sees mostly black and white. She has what is called cataracts, and they are inoperable." He sighed deeply. "She has only a few weeks left, living here in Weldona. She will be moving to a place for the elderly. She's not able to live on her own any longer."

Embarrassing tears began to form in my eyes. Then I became agitated. "I've got to do something!"

"There's nothing you can do," Dad said comfortingly. "She's going blind, but she will be well taken care of."

"No, I mean about sunsets. I have to help her see a sunset. That's why she invited me over. Don't you see?"

Dad didn't see. "But that's just what you did, Son."

"No, I didn't do a good job. I want to try it again. Last Christmas she gave me a box of 64 crayons. She hoped that I had learned some of the colors and could help her see a sunset. Well, I'm going to learn those colors. I'm going to help her see one more Colorado sunset."

"I know how we can do it," said Shirley, who had been listening intently. "I'll help you. We can make flashcards. I'll be your teacher!"

Oh great! That was just what I needed. My seven-year-old sister teaching me with flashcards!

But it *was* a good idea. That night, since it was summer and we didn't have school work, we proceeded to make flashcards out of some 3 x 5 note cards that Mom had in her office stuff. We pulled out the 64 crayon box that had hardly been used since Christmas, and picked out the colors we thought might be used to describe a sunset. On one side of the card we colored the color. On the other side we wrote the name with the same crayon. It didn't take long and by bedtime we had all the cards made. We worked on it every night for a week. *It seems that I'm a slow learner.* But with Shirley's dogged persistence, finally I had learned the colors.

It was late on a Saturday evening, and a full week had gone by, when Dad, Mom, Shirley and I pulled into Aunt Maud's driveway. She had been told that Shirley and I were bringing by a late evening 'Tea.' I didn't know it then, but later I found out that all women love Teas. It's in their make up. Until that point I had just endured Shirley's Teas. But this evening was something special. Shirley was in her element, as she laid out the quartered peanut butter and jam sandwiches (minus the crust) and the miniature tea set that Mom had given her for her birthday. Mom boiled some water in the kitchen and Shirley and Maud chattered away, as if eighty years didn't separate their ages.

I, on the other hand, was rehearsing crayon colors in my brain. I was discretely consulting my flashcards when Dad leaned over from his chair and said, "It will be all right, Son. Just say whatever comes into your heart. Don't ever let stress be a part of a sunset."

Finally the 'Tea' was over and the sun was

dipping low in the western sky. Shirley and Mom cleaned up the tea set and Dad nabbed all of the extra tiny sandwiches and quietly downed them. Then we all sat on Maud's back porch and settled in for the show.

Right on cue, Aunt Maud asked me, "Larry, could you tell me what you see?"

"Sure, Aunt Maud. The plains are dressed for the evening. The sage is olive green and the deep green cottonwood trees are a-shimmering in a feathered breeze." I looked over to Shirley. She was mouthing the words we had been rehearsing for days. "The foot hills rise in a dusty forest green. The mountains themselves are almost a charcoal gray, but bordering them, from one end of the horizon to the other, the sky is a ribbon of carnation pink. The sun itself is a red orange slipping into a red mahogany slumber."

"Oh," Maud exclaimed, "I love the sound of that!"

"The sky is a washed yellow that comes our way with aquamarine, blue green, blue gray and periwinkle. It ends in a deep, deep blue right over our heads."

Maud raised her head to the sky as if she could just the vision I had described. "What comes next, Larry?" I looked at Shirley. She looked at me. We had *definitely* not rehearsed this! I closed my eyes and forged on.

"Then, coming soon is the navy blue, the deepest, darkest blue, and the dark, dark black of night," I concluded. I opened my eyes with relief. Finally it was over.

"Yes, yes. The night is coming, isn't it?" Maud sighed. I smiled as she sighed until I saw the looks on my parents' faces. They were as dark as the night to come, and the night that was coming for Maud.

Aunt Maud said to my dad, "Marion, I think I will let you take me inside tonight." Dad took her arm and gently led her in. She paused at the door to the kitchen and said, "Larry, I will keep that description and all of those colors in my memory for ever. Thank you."

That was the last time I ever saw Aunt Maud. Within two weeks she went back to be with her children in her home state of Iowa.

I was spending an afternoon with my grandsons recently. I had just given them a 64 pack of crayons and some coloring books. After a few minutes, something else caught their attention and they tumbled out of the room. On the floor, I saw broken, mangled and mashed crayons. I knelt down and carefully started collecting them. I tried to straighten the broken, realign the mangled, and re-form the mashed into the box. I was taken back to a time, fifty-six years earlier, when my little sister held up flash cards and drilled me endlessly. The laughing. The giggling. My whole body smiled as I looked at the box on the floor. There were colors missing. The box was crunched. But, in some way, it took me back to my childhood in Weldona.

The old name isn't used any more, but the color I miss the most is "Indian Red," because that was the color that brought an old woman and a little boy together for a lifetime of sunsets.

THREE MEN ON A SLAB

by Larry Wayne Miller

A merciful God has pity for men who work by the sweat of their brows and the hardness of their hands. In the very deepest heat of the day, He created...*night*.

After a hot, grueling day of pouring concrete, Dad and I were driving toward a cheap motel for the night. We were looking forward to a cool shower, followed by a trip to a nearby diner for supper, and at last, a well-deserved night of rest, punctuated by my dad's snores. Hopefully all of that was mere moments away, but right at that moment, I was singing at the top of my lungs.

Dad looked on with a bewildered smirk while I sang the lyrics of Johnny Cash's latest hit, *Ring of Fire*. It was playing on the radio, one of the few things that actually worked in our spartan excuse for a farm truck. The truck in question was a 1955 International Harvester, a heavy duty pick-up with big mud tires. It had heavy overload springs and an I-beam front axle, which made it feel like sitting on a brick in an earthquake. The only ventilation was provided by wing vents that sucked in an amazing amount of hot air, bugs, wasps, and an occasional 'slow bird.' This made it very noisy, hence 'the top of my lungs' stuff. But the truck was dependable and 'bulletproof.'

Dad leaned against the driver's door of the truck, steering with his fingertips, while I leaned on the other door. He was turned slightly my way, trying to figure out what had come over me at the end of a very long and exhausting day.

I grinned, rolled down *my* window, and belted out the chorus into the Colorado night.

This long and exhausting day had started at five a.m. on a blisteringly hot day in June of 1965. I would be turning 16 in a few days. At that age, I knew that I had the confidence and the stamina to complete any work thrown my way. Grandpa Miller said I was full of something (which I was not allowed to say at home) and vinegar. Mom was scandalized, but Grandpa was correct. I was also full of barely controlled sweat, hormones, attitude and…all of the other things Grandpa had said. Anyway, Dad was always looking for ways to bring in extra cash to supplement the meager farm income, so he had accepted a job of pouring and finishing a concrete slab for a church two hundred miles from home. Home, by the way, was Weldona, Colorado, right where Nebraska takes a nick out of Colorado.

After a breakfast of biscuits and gravy (three helpings worth) at a local truck stop, we had headed to the job site for a 6 a.m. pour. We had started to check the bracing of our forms so we would be totally ready, and to calm the "concrete jitters," when the big cement truck came rumbling around the corner. Concrete sometimes acts like a living thing. It flows where you don't want it. It pushes back when you are trying move it. It shows every imperfection and mistake you make, dries when it darn well pleases, and leaves a permanent record for a hundred years. As Dad often said, it was downright cantankerous, mutinous, and ornery. But on this day it had gone very well, considering that it was a large pour. Dad and I had worked on a few concrete jobs so we knew each other's moves and responsibilities, and were very efficient in getting it put to bed by 5 p.m.

Now, driving along toward that beckoning motel, we were both in our stocking feet. We had thrown our wet stinky rubber boots into the bed of the truck. We reeked of sweat and grime. Our clothes were caked with dry concrete. We were definitely grubby in every respect. But we were done for the day, and glad of it. Hence, my singing.

Dad turned down the radio so he could talk at a normal level, or perhaps it was simply self-preservation.

"I'm surprised you're a Johnny Cash fan, uh, a

country and western fan, I guess you call it," he said, at an elevated volume.

I answered in kind. "Actually I'm not. It's just that 'country' is all this truck seems to play." I looked over at him and grinned. He grinned right back.

"Maybe I could find some Elvis for you," he said, reaching for the tuner knob.

I started to say something pithy, but thought better of it when I realized he was genuinely trying to please me. I beat him to the knob and turned the radio all the way off.

"Actually, I'm more of a Beatles guy." He looked blank.

"You know, 'She Loves You,' and, 'I Wanna Hold Your Hand.' Those guys?"

He harrumphed, and turned his attention back to the road. "You mean those boys with long hair, on the Ed Sullivan Show?"

"That's the ones," I affirmed.

We drove on in silence for awhile... well, as silent as you could get in a noisy farm truck. We hadn't heard of white noise back then. Our *whole world* was white noise.

After a few more miles I said, "Actually, Dad, I'm starting to get a little hungry."

He let out a big contagious laugh. "Well, *there's* a big surprise." I waited for more. "We still have part of a box of donuts and some cold coffee in a thermos, don't we, Son?"

"Yum, yum," I mocked.

"Well, it will have to do until we get back to the mot...."

I looked over to see why he had stopped in mid-sentence. I saw him looking to the right. I followed his gaze and spotted a construction site. It was much like the one we had just left. Too much like it, in fact! There was an old white church surrounded by large gnarled cottonwood trees and in its midst was a lone man on his hands and knees, running a trowel over quickly drying concrete.

Dad slowed down and pulled the truck to the side of the road. He shut off the engine. He leaned his huge forearms on the steering wheel and got that *look* on his face.

I knew that *look*. It meant we were probably going to be later, and dirtier, and even more exhausted before bed time, and we were *definitely* going to miss dinner.

I closed my eyes and concentrated on stifling my anger. By the age of 15 I had been through this a hundred times. Dad would *never* pass someone in need. It drove me crazy.

"Son," he said, quietly.

I kept my eyes closed. Maybe he would change his mind or modify his plan if I waited it out. Then I felt tears brim my eyes. I was so frustrated and so tired. Tired and frustrated... but not angry. I knew how this would turn out. We were going to spend hours helping someone out of a jam. That's just the way it was in our family.

Over the last few months, I had mellowed. I understood what Dad was made of and I was beginning to think I was made of the same stuff. *But still....* I was looking forward to an evening removed from work…and our room had a *color* TV!

"Son," Dad said, again.

I rubbed back my tears with the backs of my hands, and looked at Dad. He could be tough when he needed to be. He could be opinionated and obstinate. But there were other days, like today, when he could be intuitive, and knowing, and even gentle.

"This is not my call," he said. "I've been running your life since 1949. Just look over at that job site and tell me what you see. If you say, 'Let's go home,' that is exactly what we'll do. I'm just as tired as you are. It wouldn't hurt my feelings at all to go back to the motel, take a long shower, and go eat masses of greasy burgers and fries." He grinned. I grinned back, weakly.

I looked over at the job site. It looked to be an addition to an old church. It was much like the one we had just come from. The top soil had been carefully moved to the side. The batter boards were expertly and carefully constructed. There was the remains of a pile of #4 rebar, which meant that it would be a strong slab.

"Words, Son. I need words. Time's a-wasting."

Without taking my eyes off the job site, I said, "It was a big pour. Thirty by forty I would say. About fifteen yards. The surface is beginning to chalk up. He doesn't have much time and I don't see any help."

I looked at the man on the slab. He looked to be in his seventies. He had a long way to go until he was done. A long and painful way, at the rate he was going.

"So, what do you say?" Dad queried.

"I say - help..." I swallowed hard, and cleared my throat. "I say, help is on the way!"

Dad started up the truck and pulled into the site, next to the man's old Ford 150. There was an old tool trailer behind it, stuffed with tools of the trade.

We were putting on our smelly boots, slipping on our dirty knee pads, and unloading our trowels, when the man turned to see what was going on.

Dad was a man of few words, so he went to the slab, got on his knees, and began smoothing out the rough concrete with a magnesium trowel. I got the edger and began knocking down the side of the slab. The man seemed to know what was happening but was still flabbergasted by it. Dad, sensing the stare, and without taking his eyes off the trowel, said, "My name is Marion Miller. This is my son, Larry."

The man stood, speechless, while precious seconds ticked away. Finally he spoke. "I'm Bob." And still, he stood and he stared.

"We're here to take the place of the men who didn't come," Dad said.

"How - how did you know about them?"

Dad seemed to be annoyed by the multitude of words so I answered. "You are clearly a good planner. All of your lumber and rebar is in neat piles. Your batter boards are well laid out and your forms are well braced. Your job shack is even recently painted. I'm sure you had help coming. They're just not here yet."

Bob returned to his work and grumbled, "They aren't coming at all." With that we all returned to the job at hand.

I turned to the slab and started to work the large

rocks down, allowing the cement and the sand to come to the surface, which I worked into a nice smooth edge. I had a long ways to go. It was over 140 feet around the perimeter.

Soon my sore muscles released their resentment at being treated so harshly twice in the same day, and remembered the joy and sense of accomplishment in taking a raw piece of pliable concrete and turning it into something that would endure a hundred years.

It took over an hour to work my way around the big slab. The last twenty feet had started to set up and I had to beat it into place with a wood trowel. Meanwhile Dad and Bob had reached a silent agreement. Bob worked the edges of the slab with a small bull float with a steel trowel and Dad worked the center with our old magnesium bull float with a twenty foot handle.

Since I finished first, I went in search of something to eat. The dried-out donuts and cold coffee were sitting in the truck. I put them on the tailgate of our International Harvester. Bob showed up a few minutes later with two bananas, half a loaf of bread, and, glory be, a jar of peanut butter.

He held up the peanut butter and said, "I always keep this for *concrete* emergencies." Ha! Ha!

Dad, just joining the party, said, "That's practically what this boy survives on." We all laughed the laugh of people who know how to work hard and share a tough common goal. Half way through our snack, I remembered the story of the fishes and the loaves, from Sunday School. We broke what we had into small amounts, and by the time we drank the last of the cold coffee, we were full and satisfied. For the moment, at least.

"I don't know what I would've done if you fellers hadn't shown up," Bob sighed, a faraway look on his face.

"We just happened by at the right time," Dad replied.

"In the nick of time," Bob added. "But, what made you stop and help?"

"It wasn't my choice," Dad beamed. "It was at Larry's prompting. It was his call." I felt my face burning.

Bob turned to me and said, "Well, I thank you mightily, young man." More burning. He stuck out his hand and we shook. Then he turned to Dad and they shook hands, too.

Just then an older model Cadillac pulled up. Inside was a burly man smoking a cigar. He threw the cigar on the ground and opened the door, ponderously unfolding himself from the Caddie. He was, well, to put it nicely, he was *very* large…in every direction. He was wearing the kind of narrow tie that was fashionable at the time, and an open double-breasted suit that was a few sizes too small. My first impression was that of a marshmallow. He had no corners, no angles. His hands were soft. His features were soft. He leaned against the car door and said, "How's it going, young man?"

At first I thought he was talking to me, but then I saw Bob roll his eyes and look away. The light-hearted greeting was meant for him! He had heard this one-sided banter before.

The big man blustered on, talking to Bob's back, "Anything you need, Bob?"

Bob turned and with sarcasm dripping from his voice said, "Yeah, you could deliver those two experienced volunteers you promised me."

A dead silence ensued as the big man turned pink, then red, and finally, deep purple. "Well, you see, that's why, ahhhh, why I sorta... dropped by. You see...They're... Not... Coming."

Bob gave the big man a stare that only a seventy year old retired carpenter who has survived the Great Depression, the Dust Bowl, and World War II could give to a man who had never worked with his hands for a day in his life. "No kidding, Sherlock," Bob fumed. "How long ago did you find out?"

Man shrugged, put on a cheesy grin, and said, "Well, ahhh, I found out at lunch. But I've been in meetings all afternoon and this is the first chance I've had to get here. And," he said in a self-righteous tone, "I did call the church phone. No one answered."

"Maybe that was because the only man who ever answers the church phone was right here, doing the work of three men," Bob replied.

Big Man had no comeback. He was out of ammunition. But, gesturing to Dad and me, he squeaked, "At least you found these men."

"First of all, I didn't find them, they found me. And secondly, they are not men. They are angels, sent from God."

Dad and I had heard enough. We returned to cleaning our tools, stifling a snicker all the while.

The big man sighed. "The offer still stands." He

started the laborious process of folding himself back into the old Cadillac.

"There is one thing even *you* can do," Bob called.

"And what would that be?"

"Bring these men lots of burgers and fries….. and I do mean *lots*! And bring some for me. Lots!"

Big Man drove off in a huff and a cloud of blue smoke. Bob turned to Dad and me and said, "Don't ask. Don't even ask."

The sun was setting as we positioned the two trucks with their headlights turned on, to illuminate as much of the slab as possible. Bob asked Dad to run his old power trowel because, at his age, he explained, his eyes didn't do well at night. We spent the next hour putting the slab to bed. I went around the whole perimeter with the edger, Bob used a steel trowel, and Dad ran the power trowel. I thought the sound of the Briggs and Stratton engine purring into the Colorado night had to be about the sweetest lullaby imaginable.

We cleaned up our trowels, boots, and tools, and were putting them away for the second time that day when Bob walked over. "I'd like to pay you fellers, but the two that didn't show up were supposed to be volunteers. In fact, I'm a volunteer. I go to this church. We're all pitching in to make this here Fellowship Hall."

"We didn't do this for money," Dad replied.

"I know you didn't," Bob said. "Fact is, this is my last job. I'm hanging it up after tonight." Dad and I just listened for more of the story. Bob, sensing he had our attention, continued on. "I'm a Christian." He looked to us for some kind of confirmation. Dad nodded. So did I.

"I'm also a praying man." He again looked to us for a response. Again, we nodded.

"I thought so," he said. "I've been a contractor, slash, farmer my whole life." He smiled at the thought of his next words. "You might say I'm a contractor so I can pay for my hobby, which is farming."

We both smiled at the old joke. "So what I'm getting at is..." Bob was obviously at a loss for words. "Is..." He sat on the tailgate and looked Dad in the eye. "I've been praying that someone would come along who would appreciate carpenter tools as much as I do. I have daughters and *none* of their husbands want my old tools. I've approached some of the young men in this church and none of them are interested. So last night and today while I was waiting for the help that never came, I asked God to send me someone else to help, someone who understood tools and respected them." His eyes moistened, and he said, "Then God sent you." Pause. "You two are meant to have my tools."

Dad took a step back, like he had been shocked. I just stared. Bob motioned to the trailer behind his truck. "Will you do this old man the honor of honoring his tools?"

Dad looked at the trailer full of tools, and I followed suit. There was a cement mixer, the power trowel that Dad had just used, and several bull floats. There were steel trowels all over the place. That was just what we could see!

Dad stood up, walked over to Bob, shook his hand and said, "It would be my honor, sir."

The two men were still gripping each other's hands when the big Cadillac drove back in. The big man didn't even try to get out. He just rolled down the window and motioned me to come over. I did, and he thrust food boxes and large cups of soda at me. He drove off, tires spitting gravel at us, hurrying on his way to his next big thing.

That night, we three ate our supper on the tailgate of the old International Harvester farm truck. What a sight we must have been - three filthy dirty, thoroughly exhausted men, chugging down large soft drinks, hamburgers, and fries, under the soft summer moon, listening to the Beatles on the radio.

Within less than a year my father was beginning a new career that would see him build over 100 churches all over the United States, Central America, and the Caribbean. He spent the last ten years of his life building churches, colleges, and orphanages in Africa. And yes, he used some of Bob's tools in all those places. Today, I still use them.

GREEN CAR BLUE

by Larry Wayne Miller

"Whatdayathink? Whatdayathink?!"

Dad, who could revert to a *ten year old boy*, complete with pre-adolescent run-on vernacular, had just done so, in an instant, in front of Mom, my eight-year-old sister Shirley, and myself - who just happened to *be* a ten year old boy. I loved it! This was the fun side of my Dad. His arms were stretched wide, as if we were expected to embrace whatever he had discovered, invented, or created. His grin was as wide as the Cheshire Cat's, and he pulsated with a youthful expectant excitement that was just a scratch beneath the surface of this veteran, weathered, gritty farmer.

It was the summer of 1959 and I welcomed these occasional outbursts. They gave me a peek into the soul of the man who could work harder, longer, and in more challenging conditions than any other man I knew - a man who believed that work is a virtue to be nurtured and cultivated just like the soil he tilled every day - a man who also happened to be my father. But more importantly for me, his antics meant there would be a slight respite from the hard, demanding work that life on a farm involved - a little downtime, so to speak.

Over Dad's shoulder I could see our bright red barn, a leaning concrete silo, and a field of corn two feet high. All of this was framed by a brilliant blue northeast Colorado sky. Cotton candy clouds and green-leafed cottonwood trees shimmered in the evening breeze.

What Mom saw didn't exist beyond the back of Dad's head. She had seen this look before. To her it meant that Dad thought he had some brilliant whiz-bang idea that was going to garner instant cash-money. He had invented something, redesigned some piece of machinery, or he had found a diamond in the rough. His experimenting and maneuvering had never brought in any real money, so Mom was more than a little skeptical when 'The Look' showed its cheesy grin. I knew all this just by looking at her face, because I had heard her say these things over and over again, sometimes behind his back, sometimes right in front of his face.

I had to smile in spite of myself. It was the exact same scene I had watched on television just the night before, right in our living room! But it hadn't been my mom and dad as the principal players then, it had been "The Honeymooners" on television.

"Well? Well? What do you think?" Now, Dad was a little more subdued. He was becoming slightly anxious at the lack of response and the look on my mother's face. In an attempt to win her over, he continued, "Well, come on, I'll show you what I just bought." With that he turned and pointed us toward the farmyard. It was then we saw it. It was a drab green Chevy sedan with a large white star on the door.

"It's an Army car. I just bought it at auction. Isn't it great!?" he beamed.

It wasn't great, it was awful! Anybody with half a brain could see that. It was drab green and it was old. As a boy, I poured over car magazines, and knew the look of every era by heart. I was guessing by its swept back appearance that it was a World War II Army sedan. But anyway, we didn't need a car, especially an old car. We already had a cushy '53 De Soto, and it met our needs just fine.

"It's an ugly green," Shirley blurted out in her customary frankness.

"Why, yes, it is," Dad said in the manner of a used car salesman about to lose a sale. "But you see, Shirley, that's because it is an *Army* car, and *Army* cars are supposed to be olive green, which, I admit, is kind of ugly."

"And it has a big white star on the door," Shirley deadpanned.

"Yes...yes, it does," Dad said, clearly nervous about the outcome. "That is because it is a car made for a *General*. A *General* car. Get it? It's a *General Motors* car made for a *General*."

Ba Da Boom! The natives were restless.

"So why did you buy it?" Mom said, at last. I guess she knew the answer, as it was *always* the same answer.

Dad hemmed and hawed. Finally, he said, sheepishly, "For an investment."

Mom apparently decided not to continue this argument in front of the children. "For now," she said, with some authority, "would you please take your investment and park it somewhere else." She walked back into the house, her domain.

Dad stood in his domain, which was everything outside of the house. He was bewildered and confused. The look on his face said that he had thought his new purchase would be received with open and adoring arms.

He said to us kids, "It only cost fifty bucks." I nodded. Shirley hesitated, just a little, but still nodded. With that he walked back to the *Army* car, mumbling about needing to check the registration. He started it, and drove it behind the big red barn.

When he got back from the barn, Dad decided to change the subject. He asked me, "So, would you like to help me go and bring back the International 400 from the Home Place?" *Would I!*

"You bet!" was my immediate answer. I had only been able to drive Grandpa's big International tractor on two other occasions, and this would give me a chance to enjoy it the entire four miles back to our place.

"How about me?" Shirley asked, "Can I come too?" She had always loved machines, every bit as much as I did.

"I'm sorry, Sis," Dad said. He almost always called her Sis. "Your mother said you still have chores to do, in the house." Clearly disappointed, and with her lip sticking out, she trudged back to the house.

As Dad and I drove away, I noticed that Mom and Shirley were back outside, standing together watching and waving to us as we left. That was odd! I could never remember Mom watching us as we went off to work.

I sat in the driver's seat of the International on a couple folded-up feed sacks. Even though I was supposed to be paying 100 percent of my attention to driving, I found myself drifting into thoughts of the events of this day. I hated it when Mom and Dad had differences of opinion. But I was old enough to realize that was pretty much the fate of husbands and wives the world over, or at least in my 'neck of the woods.' I knew that Dad meant well. I also knew that he felt he had the right to do something for himself on occasion. But more than once, I had heard Uncle Roy say, "My brother needs to choose his spots a little better."

An hour or so later, when I drove the tractor into the farmyard, I noticed that there were two blue cars in the driveway, and that Mom was talking to two men. I knew them to be a neighboring farmer, Mr. Hoover, and his son. I parked the tractor next to the silo, quite proud of myself for how well I did it.

Dad parked his truck. He introduced the two men to Mom and Shirley, who were standing by the house watching the scene unfold.

"We already met," Shirley informed Dad. I knew them already. We shared a fence, up north.

Dad said to all assembled, "I'll go get it. You *will* be greatly impressed." With that he shuffled off around the corner of the barn. A moment later he walked back around the barn empty-handed, with a look of bewilderment on his face. He walked purposefully, heading straight at Mom. His eyes were as fiery as I had ever seen, and still he walked toward my mother. Then just as he finally approached her, his face softened a bit. The look that came over him said, *'Maybe there is something I don't understand. Perhaps there is a reasonable explanation.'*

With excruciating control he said, "Where is my car?"

Mom didn't answer.

Dad said again, punctuating each word, "Where. Is. My. Car?" An uncomfortable silence ensued.

He was getting ready to ask again with more force, but then Shirley blurted out, "Green car blue." She pointed towards the blue car parked next to our neighbor's Ford.

Dad looked in stunned disbelief at Shirley's hand, itself a bright shade of blue. He stood motionless. His mouth fell open as the realization of what her blue hand meant dawned on him. All of us, except Dad, quickly looked at the now blue Chevy. It was obvious that it had been hastily painted with a bristly old paint brush. Maybe two bristly old paintbrushes. There were streaks of paint on the doors, and the faint image of a large star.

Dad, not having moved an inch, began to quiver. "I...There...It was...How could you...I was selling it for money...as an antique, rare, *Army car*....for a profit!"

Mom stood up straight and said, "Marion, you should have told me that. I'm not a mind reader, you know. I was actually trying to help you out of an embarrassing situation." Then she folded her arms and stood waiting for the next part of the scene.

Shirley raised her little blue hand, pointed her little blue finger and chirped, "I'm not a mind reader either." (Actually she was. That is, she was an uncanny personality reader. But that is a different story for a different time.)

Dad raised his hand, index finger pointed to the sky, and prepared for his soliloquy. He never got the chance. Behind Dad, Mr. Hoover chuckled, then he laughed, and then he guffawed. Then he said, with mirth dripping from his eyes, "Green Car Blue. That's a good one. I'll have to tell that to the boys." With that, he motioned to his son and they chuckled all the way to their car. (I knew that "boys" was a colloquial diversion that meant he was going to tell *everyone* in the valley.)

As soon as our guests had driven out of the driveway, Dad, looking florid and despondent, said, "I was going to sell that for three hundred dollars. They had the cash! It is a very rare car that had been used by one of the most important generals in the Denver area, back during the war. Do you know what it is worth now?"

I shrugged. Shirley shrugged. Mom winced.

Three hundred dollars was a fortune in those days. I said, "Less?"

He looked at the car. Then he looked at us. "Now it is worth nothing. N-O-T-H-I-N-G. Nothing." He stood silently for a few moments. Then the corner of his mouth began to curl up, ever so slightly. His eyes began to glisten. His huge shoulders began to vibrate as he tried to stifle a giggle, looking as if he had to sneeze. Finally the innate humor of the situation got the best of him and tears of relief coursed his cheeks.

He looked at Shirley. "Green Car Blue," he laughed. "That *is* a good one!"

Suddenly Shirley took Dad's farmer pose, her little index finger pointed to the sky. She took on the veneer of Alice Cramden of the Honeymooners, and said, in a whiny voice, "Ralph, it would help if you would just communicate, once in a while."

Going with the moment, Dad assumed a similar pose and uttered the lines that made Ralph Cramden one of the most beloved curmudgeons of 1950's sitcoms. "One of these days, Alice," His finger began to vibrate as he thrust it to the sky, "To the Mooooooooon!!!"

Eventually, Dad sold the blue car for a little more than he'd paid for it. The fallout from this little saga followed us for quite a few months, right into the winter. Every time we went to the local market or were on our way into church, people would exclaim, with mirth in their eyes, "GREEN CAR BLUE!"

THE LEROY RULE

by Larry Wayne Miller

"Larry, look at your new shirt!"

I *knew* that was what Mom would say. I just knew it! As soon as I got a teeny tiny bit of tractor grease on my brand new store-bought shirt I said to myself, "Self! You are going to get busted for this!"

Yep. Word for word. Busted!

It had all started on a Sunday, in August of 1960. I was eleven years old. We lived in the small town of Weldona in the northeastern corner of Colorado. Just the day before, Mom had taken me shopping. We drove to Fort Morgan, thirty miles away, to buy one of the first new shirts of my young life.

Most of my clothing, up to that point, came from a hand-me-down box that arrived, regular as clockwork, on my birthday - every June. The other things that arrived every birthday were: socks from my Grandmother Conner, underwear from my Grandmother Miller, work boots from my parents, and mouthwash from Great Aunt Maud. Boy, I looked forward to birthdays!

"Just look at that shirt, and at your shoes!" Mom shrieked.

I looked. Dirt mixed with grease. On the bottoms. Of my shoes. Oh My!

"You're just like your father."

Actually, I liked being like my father. He was a great guy. But he had the same short- sightedness, when it came to clean clothing. All of the time.

"Go back outside. Clean up your shoes. Take off your shirt. Then carry them to the back porch. Then come into the kitchen. I want to talk to you."

Ouch! The talk. In the kitchen. No shirt. No shoes. No escape.

When I was outside cleaning up and taking off my greasy clothes, I could see Dad doing some light chores in his Sunday best. He looked over at me in my state of humiliating undress. Then he slowly turned and looked at the two buckets of grain he was holding, one in each hand. Then he looked at his pants. I could read his mind, one hundred feet away.

BUSTED!

As I walked back into the kitchen, Mom intoned the obvious, "Larry, you are almost twelve years old."

Good start. No yelling. No, "You're grounded." Putting the ball squarely back in my court.

"Well, technically, I just turned eleven two months ago. But I guess that makes me 'almost twelve,' " I said, not knowing where this was going.

Undaunted, my mother continued, "I don't want to clean up after you any more!"

I should have run it through my measly filter, but instead I said, "You clean up after Dad, all of the time."

Mom tilted her head and quizzically looked a hole straight through me, as if to say, 'Are you really that obtuse?'

Of course if she *had* said it, I would have thought she was talking about excessive weight gain. Instead, she regrouped and forged on.

"Look at your Uncle Roy. Look at your grandfather, for that matter. They are always clean, pressed, and patched."

"How about Dad?" I inquired defensively.

Mom lifted her eyes to the heavens, and exclaimed, "Lord knows I have tried!"

It was true. Marion E. Miller, my father, was a dust magnet. Grandma Miller said he could walk into a room and every bit of dust and grease would magically leave the room attached to his overalls.

"Who do you think washes, presses, mends, and patches the clothes these men wear?" Mom continued.

"Women folk," I blurted. "But that's what you do."

Easy boy! Bad choice of words. Terrible timing.

Mom looked like a tea kettle left on high heat,

ready to explode.

I tried to make amends and sputtered on, "And we're grateful. We are so really, really grateful. And…and, I know, that, ah, I wouldn't, ah, want your job. No. No, no, no. I'll deal with the heavy stuff and…"

Mom broke in, "From now on you will deal with *all* of the stuff." She folded her arms and leaned on the kitchen table.

Suddenly I felt quite vulnerable. What with no shirt, no shoes, and now, no laundry service.

"From now on you will wash your own clothes, dry your own clothes, mend your own clothes, and press your own clothes." She stood up after her momentous pronouncement and left the room with a satisfied smile on her face.

I sat there realizing one phase of my life was over and another was about to begin. Dad had taught me many lessons about personal responsibility in my public life. Now Mom was pushing me into the more personal realm of private responsibility.

Lessons began after dinner that night. From that point on I was in charge of my own wardrobe. Mom would step up and help quite often, but I was responsible for my own clothes. It wasn't until permanent press clothing came along that all harried mothers, everywhere, got a reprieve.

During the next weeks Mom taught me how to darn socks, mend tears in my clothing, and sew on effective patches. Washing clothes and hanging them out to dry had been in my repertoire for quite a few years. By the time the wounds in my fingers had begun to heal (from a few sock darning episodes) Mom had me ironing my shirts and pants. Although it did have to be folded, underwear was allowed to crumple. Thank goodness! Besides, Mom said she thought men handling undergarments was a little weird.

The last lesson wasn't taught by Mom. It was a lesson that needed to be taught by observation. It was the lesson of how to look crisp when everyone around you looked soggy.

Even I understood that Marion E. Miller wasn't going to be my teacher. He was a hard worker and a great teacher of everything from how to work with tools to how to work the fields. But a clothier, he was not. And Mom was smart enough to realize that I was beginning to chafe under her instruction, so teaching me that ultimately important lesson needed to fall to a man who had impeccable credentials.

Enter Albert Leroy Miller, my dad's younger brother. He was tall, good looking, well- spoken and always well-attired. When he walked into a room and women were in attendance, there would be a severe case of, as my grandfather would call it, 'swivel heads.'

We always called him Uncle Roy. He was the object of my assignment and I wasted no time getting to the bottom of what it was like to be...'Roy.' Dad and I stopped by a field of corn Uncle Roy was planting to see if he could help us purchase some seed corn. Uncle Roy was an agent for a leading seed manufacturer and one of the valley's main suppliers of seed corn.

While Dad and Uncle Roy were standing near the tractor, talking, I discreetly went around to the passenger side and rummaged through his 1958 Chevy half-ton pickup for clues of his continually presentable appearance. His lunch box was on the seat. It looked like a black covered wagon without the wheels. Next to it was an extra tall thermos of coffee. One thermos would barely get a person through the morning, let alone the whole day, as Dad would constantly remind anyone who would listen.

The glove box contained no gloves but did have an extra pair of pliers and a small pocket knife, two tools a farmer was never without. Next to them were surveyor maps, and of course, duct tape.

No clues there. So I tipped the back of the seat forward, to see the space behind where tools were often kept. There was a bottle jack, a tire wrench, and a few other assorted tools in a small homemade tool box. Then I spied something! Tucked in behind the bottle jack, I saw some denim, rolled up with a piece of baling string, which was wrapped around and tied in a neat bow. I leaned closer to get a better view. It looked to be…a…a….

"May I help you find something?"

I shot out of there, slammed the bench seat back into place, stood at attention, blinking wildly, like a deer caught in headlights.

There, framed in the driver's door, stood my Uncle Roy, resting his hands on the door post, and stooping slightly so he could see through the opening.

He said, with a quizzical look on his face, "Is there something I can help you find?"

For a moment I considered evasion and denials but immediately decided against that. Uncle Roy had always been one of my biggest supporters, and even in my youthful indiscretions had always been an encourager and mentor. I had always been a terrible liar and he would have seen right through me, instantly, leaving a question in his mind that might never have been answered.

So I chose the honesty approach. "Mom told me to find out what you do. And do the same."

That changed the whole direction of the inquiry. He straightened to his full 6'2" and considered the context. What did I mean by, 'doing what he did', and why did I have to look behind the seat of the truck to find it? Why would his sister-in-law, my mother, send *me* to stealthily procure something she could have easily received by simply asking?

It was no secret that Grandpa Miller kept a pipe and a can of Prince Albert tucked deep into the glove box of his 1957 Chevrolet Apache pickup. My first clandestine smoking experience (and also my last) was out behind the barn, thanks to my pilfering Grandpa's stash. So I wasn't looking for *that*.

I wasn't a closet drinker, and neither was Uncle Roy. So it wasn't *that*.

None of the Miller men I knew were into girly magazines, although Grandpa kept a couple of pin-up calendars from the 1940's on his garage walls. We all enjoyed spending time in Grandpa's garage. But no, it wasn't *that*, either.

Uncle Roy was quite a thinker, and I could see that this thinking thing could take some time. So I decided to tell the truth, the whole truth, and nothing but the truth. "Mom says you are always clean, well-mended, and well-pressed, and I am supposed to find out how you do it."

His furrowed brow turned to astonishment, and then to mirth. Then the corners of his laughing eyes preceded the question, "She *did*, did she?"

"She said to find out the secret to your constant cleanliness."

Uncle Roy left the truck window and leaned on the hood. It was an unspoken invitation to do the same. All the men of the Valley made their important decisions gathered around the hood of some old truck. It was their board room on the prairie.

Uncle Roy continued, "And you thought you would find the secret behind the seat, or maybe in the glove box?"

"Actually when you say it that way, it sounds rather silly," I confessed.

About that time Dad, curious about the delay, came over and joined us. Uncle Roy made room for him and said to me, "Everything you just said doesn't have anything to do with us." He motioned to himself and my dad. "But it does have everything to do with the women in our lives. Your grandma Miller didn't raise us to be slobs. We can do that quite naturally ourselves. She started off each day well-fed with the food you eat, and with food from the Good Book.

"No matter how tough times were, we were well-mended and clean. She expected us to come into the house at the end of each day in a similar fashion. She had a back porch built onto the home place just so all the men would have a place to clean up and change into clean clothes, or at least a place to get out of their overalls.

"Your aunt Darlene and your mom do the same. They start us off clean, well mended and pressed every morning. What we do the rest of the day is up to us. I just keep emergency clothes for every occasion rolled up behind the seat along with a few toiletries and a first aid kit, so that I'm always ready to change a tire, bandage a cut, or go to a co-op meeting in a moment's notice. It's just a matter of always being ready for any situation."

This conversation was taking place in the sixties and Uncle Roy's next observation reflected that.

"What you need to remember, Larry, is that in spite of the popularity of beatniks and such like, dirty and raggedy isn't cool or hip. It's just plain dirty and raggedy."

As soon as Dad got home, he discreetly rolled up some extra clothes, wrapped some bailing twine around them, and put them behind the seat of the old Chevy truck. I don't remember him ever using them, but hey, it's the thought that counts, right?

I have similar bundles in my trucks these days, and they have saved me from a fate worse that...well, the ire of a loved one, on many an occasion. To this day, fifty-some years later, I govern my clothier decisions by the 'Leroy Rule.'

PLOWING FOR CHRISTMAS

by Larry Wayne Miller

It was cold. Cold to the bone cold. An incessant northwesterly blow brought frigid Canadian air down through Montana and Wyoming so that by the time it reached our house in northeastern Colorado, nothing in its path could stay warm. Cattle turned their backs on it and huddled in small, motionless groups, warmed only by their breath and what heat remained in their frost laden bodies. Horses stood against the arctic onslaught, bowing their heads between their front legs as their nostrils emitted a frosty mist that meandered around their legs and across the frozen Colorado plain.

We waited out the first major winter storm and looked forward to sharing the joys of Christmas in a few days. The song of the wind beat against makeshift plastic storm windows and the uneven rhythm was punctuated by a banging screen door. A dry summer and a slim harvest would make this a lean holiday. With just a few days until Christmas we had yet to buy any presents. I was twelve and my sister Shirley was ten. We knew times were tough. A few days earlier Shirley had found a nicely shaped tumbleweed that we brought into the house and used as our Christmas tree.

We had wrapped a few of last year's presents just in case there was no miracle. We were raised believing in miracles and as the blessed day approached, we thought this would be a great time to see our first. We decorated the substitute tree with popcorn and handmade ornaments, but no Christmas lights this year. Dad worked long hours. He was depressed by his inability to provide a proper Christmas for the family and was earnestly seeking any kind of work that would bring in funds that would get us through the season.

Three days before Christmas, our landlord, old man Milander, called Dad. It was late, already past bed time. But he was our landlord, so he could call any time. We had a sharecropping agreement with him. He had been one of the first settlers in the valley, and the Milander clan owned or controlled one quarter of the valley.

Dad was speaking into the telephone. "You want me to plow forty acres, south of the old home place? Now?" That's a strange request, I thought. No one plowed in the dead of winter. "Oh, you want me to plow under the few inches of snow that fell a couple days back, eh?" That *almost* made sense – a way to get some vital moisture into the soil. "All right, I'll do it,"

Dad said, and hung up. Immediately, Dad went and put on two more pairs of wool socks, a second pair of pants, two more shirts, overalls, a fleece-lined leather hat, and both wool and leather mittens. He gave Mom a hug and told her not to wait up.

For the next hour, I watched through the window as Dad gassed up the tractor, built a makeshift tent over the tractor engine with a canvas irrigation dam and put a small butane heater under it to get the crankcase oil warm enough to start the engine the next morning.

Even later, as I lay in bed, I could hear Dad struggling with the canvas against the wind in his effort to secure it for the night. I fell asleep before he was finished. My last thought was wondering if I would ever have the grit to work in those kinds of conditions. If I could, then I would know I was a man.

Mom woke me up earlier than usual the next morning. I looked out through my frosted windows to see the naked cottonwood trees bending deeply in the wind, and silhouetted in the yard light against the big red barn. It wouldn't be sun-up for at least two hours, but I had to start chores early because Dad had already left to start plowing. Mom helped me, and we finished in time for a bowl of hot cereal, a quick change to school clothes, and a sprint to catch the bus at the end of the lane.

In the bus, on our way to school, we passed the field Dad was working. Mercifully, no one could tell who this madman was that was plowing on December 23. I didn't volunteer any information.

When I got home, Mom gave me a snack and told

me to dress very warmly. Dad had left instructions to bring over the pickup with the large gas tank in the back. I was only twelve, but I had been driving tractor since I was seven and trucks since I was eight. It was not uncommon to see apparently driverless trucks going up and down the gravel road, with two tiny hands on the steering wheel and two wide eyes staring through it.

I loved to drive, so I hurried to the task. As I got close to where Dad that was, I could see the old "Minneapolis U" working hard, pulling the double bottom plow against the partially frozen ground. The tractor had a large canvas dam draped over the engine area to funnel what heat there was back to the driver. It was slightly better than nothing. Dad was hunched over so that just the top of his hat was exposed to the bone chilling cold. The sun shone brightly, but the wind chill brought the temperature down to just a few degrees above zero.

I parked the truck at the end of the field and waited for Dad to finish his run. There was no one in Weldon Valley that could get more out of a machine than my dad. As the old wheat tractor crept down the field, the front wheels bounced lightly above the ground. It reminded me of a three hundred pound football lineman, on tippy-toes. It was a sure sign that an expert driver was getting every bit of power that the old tractor could provide.

Dad looked glad to see me. But as he got closer, I could see his face was blue with cold and icicles hung from his eyebrows and sideburns. He had a piece of canvas draped around his neck and shoulders, held together with a large safety pin, to cut the wind from going through his many layers of clothing. I didn't know how he could stand it. He had already been working for ten hours.

He pulled the tractor next to the truck and I got out of the heated cab to be met by a blast of unbelievably cold air. Dad crawled into the truck and drank some hot chocolate that Mom had sent him in a thermos. I pumped gas into the old 'U,' still running, where Dad had parked it. I finished none too soon, and while I put the hose away, Dad was already on his way back to the field. It looked to me like he was one-third done. At this rate, it would be another 20 hours before he finished.

I drove home, finished chores, and then Mom, Shirley, and I took some dinner to Dad. The sun was just beginning to touch the top of the Rocky Mountains as we drove our '49 Desoto into the field. Dad already had the tractor lights on and flashed them on and off when he saw us. Nothing is more important to a farmer than to have loved ones come to where he is working. It gives him strength to make it through the day.

When Dad got off the tractor, I got on. For the next twenty minutes, I did my best to make him proud. A few times, I even got the front tires a few inches off the ground. But when Dad came back out, I was ready to go someplace warm. To this day, I don't know how he stood the cold - it is beyond my understanding. As we passed, he patted my shoulder. Not a word was said, but in a small gesture he had told me that he was proud of me. I wish I could have found a way to tell him how proud I was of him.

As Mom, Shirley, and I said prayers that night, I could hear Dad's tractor whining in the clear, Colorado night. I went to sleep hearing it, and I woke up hearing it. The sound hadn't changed, and I was glad, because even in my sleep, I had worried about him.

I got up early again for chores. It was the morning of Christmas Eve – no school today. As soon as I finished, I went to the house to eat breakfast. I stayed with my sister while Mom took my father something to eat. I felt a little guilty. I was warm, rested, and fed while Dad had been working nonstop for 27 hours.

Then I had an idea. When Mom got home, I didn't say anything. I just went outside and gassed up the Massey Harris tractor and backed up to the old, two–bottom, tumble plow parked in our Machinery Lane. We hadn't used it for two years, but it still had the crank case oil I had painted on the plowshares and the threadbare tires still had enough air in them. Since it was a tumble plow, it didn't require hydraulics. I dropped in the linchpin and connected the tumble rope to the seat. I stopped by the house and told Mom what I was going to do. She started to protest, but caught herself in mid-sentence. She looked at me a few moments, and simply said "Okay, Son. I'll bring you a lunch."

I turned with a confident air and strode to the tractor. I opened the throttle up with a majestic puff of smoke and headed down the lane to take my place next to Dad in the field. When I arrived he was just coming to the end of the row. I think for once in his life, I really surprised him. I was waiting for him to turn so I could follow him when he stood to his feet, bowed deeply as if greeting royalty, and with one sweeping gesture motioned me to take the lead.

I hated the lead! It required consistency and concentration. Dad was such a good driver, it was almost impossible to stay in front him. But nevertheless, I took the challenge, and with great difficulty, stayed ahead of him. As I finished the third row, I gladly waved him back into the lead.

An hour later, Mom and Shirley brought the gas truck. They also brought hot chocolate and peanut butter sandwiches. I loved peanut butter sandwiches. My hands were just beginning to thaw out as we walked back to our majestic steeds.

Dad and I were making good time. I could tell it wouldn't be much longer until we would finish. A couple hours later, old man Milander brought by a check, even though we weren't quite done. "Good work," he said, which was high praise, coming from him.

"Thanks for the job," Dad said. I wanted to say, 'Thanks for saving Christmas,' but I didn't, party because my mouth was too cold to talk.

Mom came by a short time later and Dad gave her the money. She and Shirley sped off to Fort Morgan, thirty-five miles away. Dad and I finished just in time to take the tractors home and do chores. After a better-than-usual supper, we all sat around our corn-cob burning stove and told stories about our favorite Christmas. As Dad thawed out from his two day ordeal, his cheeks got rosier, his stories got bigger, and we all laughed at his stupid spontaneous poems, in spite of ourselves.

Our family always opened one gift on Christmas Eve and so, it was time for the tradition to continue. Shirley and I each selected a gift under the tumbleweed tree and opened it. I got a Swiss pocketknife and Shirley got a Raggedy Ann doll. Mom and Dad said they would wait until Christmas for their gifts.

Our house was heated entirely by a pot-bellied stove. During the day we burned corn cobs and at night we burned coal. Dad put on an extra amount of coal for this special occasion and we all settled down around a warm cup of eggnog, a hot fire, and muted voices of Christmas cheer.

Dad took off his shoes as he did every night at this time. There wasn't a deodorizer in the world that could cover the smell of his feet after two solid days on a tractor. But this night, I didn't mind. This was Christmas Eve and because of his hard work, we would have a wonderful Christmas with presents, sweet potatoes, and a store- bought turkey.

Then we began to sing Christmas carols. When we finished 'Silent Night' I looked over at Dad. He was sprawled out in an old, overstuffed chair with his feet up on an overturned, five gallon bucket. His clothes were worn and dirty and he smelled of gasoline. His hands were crossed over his enormous chest, his head was back, his mouth was opened, and he was snoring lightly.

What I was ten, I wondered about Santa Claus. Well, that night, I found out something about Santa

Claus. He was five feet seven, he was worn and haggard, with a two-day growth on his face. He had patches on his clothes, snored, and his feet were smelly. Maybe your Santa has a red suit, a well trimmed beard, and gives expensive gifts, but my Santa slept through Christmas Eve. And I wouldn't have it any other way.